IMAGES
of America

LAKELAND

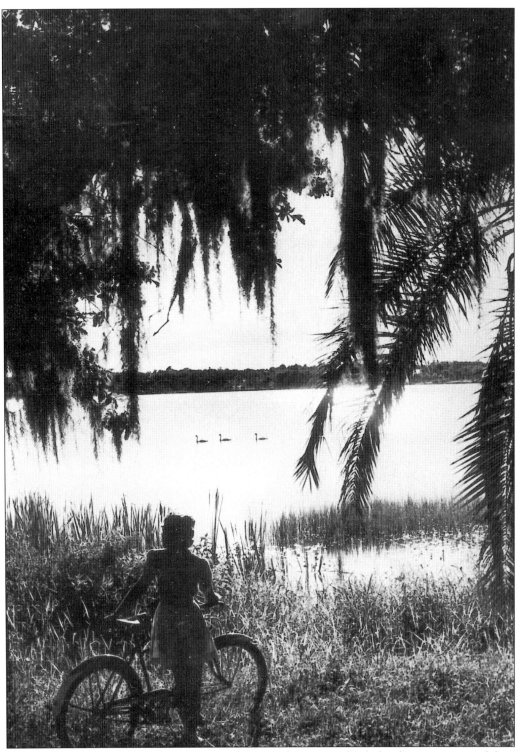
A cyclist paused for a moment of quite reflection along one of Lakeland's many scenic lakes. (Lakeland Public Library.)

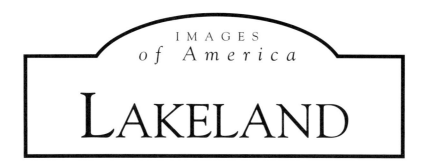

LAKELAND

Lynn M. Homan and Thomas Reilly

Copyright © 2001 by Lynn M. Homan and Thomas Reilly.
ISBN 0-7385-1398-9

Published by Arcadia Publishing,
an imprint of Tempus Publishing, Inc.
2 Cumberland Street
Charleston, SC 29401

Printed in Great Britain.

Library of Congress Catalog Card Number: 2001094685

For all general information contact Arcadia Publishing at:
Telephone 843-853-2070
Fax 843-853-0044
E-Mail sales@arcadiapublishing.com

For customer service and orders:
Toll-Free 1-888-313-2665

Visit us on the internet at http://www.arcadiapublishing.com

Contents

Acknowledgments		6
Introduction		7
1.	Uniquely Lakeland	9
2.	Places and Faces	29
3.	The Fabric of Society	49
4.	Fighting the Good Fight	69
5.	Hard at Work	89
6.	Having Fun	111

ACKNOWLEDGMENTS

We are especially grateful to Kevin Logan and Carol Juchau of the Special Collections Department of the Lakeland Public Library for both their expertise and assistance. They unfailingly answered our many questions, directed our perusal of the rich archival resources of the library, and facilitated our selection of historical images—all while assisting other library patrons, creating historical displays for the library, and designing Internet exhibits on the community's history. Their professionalism is outstanding!

Most of the photographs in this book were chosen from the historically significant photographic collections housed in the Lakeland Room at the Lakeland Public Library. Readers seeking additional images and information might also wish to consult three previously published books. *History of Polk County* by M.F. Hetherington, *Yesterday's Polk County* by Louise K. Frisbie, and Hampton Dunn's *Yesterday's Lakeland* all present various aspects of the history of Lakeland and the surrounding area.

INTRODUCTION

A few years ago, *Money* magazine ranked Lakeland as the tenth "Best Place to Live" among medium-sized cities in the South. Basing their decision on factors such as housing, crime, the economy, and the quality of life, the magazine's editors arrived at the same conclusion that the editors of the local newspaper had drawn in 1905 when they called Lakeland "Florida's Best Town." Perhaps displaying slightly less objectivity, the *Lakeland News* had described the town in glowing terms. "A place where Nature has spread her gifts with most lavish hand; where industry brings liberal rewards; where the atmosphere, both physical and moral, is pure; where the frugality and thrift of the New Englander walks hand in hand with true Southern hospitality; where extremes of heat and cold are unknown—it offers inducements to the home-builder, the health-seeker, or the investor unsurpassed by any location in the country."

Today, Lakeland offers an entrancing combination of contrasting elements that all work well together. Fields of strawberries and rolling hills covered with citrus groves surround a growing city comprised of a mixture of structures, both new and old, modern and beautifully preserved. For the architectural history buff, Lakeland offers numerous examples, including the largest single-site collection of Frank Lloyd Wright's architecture in the world. Commercial entities join with cultural organizations in mutually beneficial relationships to produce a quality of life that many other cities only hope to attain. For the artistically inclined, the city places a major emphasis on the performing and visual arts. Sports fans can cheer their favorite teams during spring training or take more active roles in water sports on the many lakes. But let us start at the beginning.

Late in 1883, Lakeland's citizens were all set to name their town Munnville in honor of Abraham G. Munn, a Kentucky businessman who had originally purchased the 80 acres upon which the town was situated. Munn declined the honor, and fortunately, alternative suggestions of Redbug and Rome City were rejected. In recognition of its many lakes, Lakeland became the name by which the small but growing Central Florida community would be known. The following year, Lakeland's founder insured the town's success when he offered the railroad acreage for right-of-way and rail facilities, as well as a lavish $2,500 railroad station.

Incorporation took place on January 1, 1885, followed by the arrival of the railroad that fall. While linking the town to the rest of Florida, rail transportation provided a dependable way of shipping local products and receiving outside goods. Realizing that the railroad would also bring travelers to Lakeland, Abraham Munn built Tremont House, the town's first hotel, at a cost of $20,000. General stores, furniture stores, and drugstores, as well as offices for doctors, lawyers, and real estate salesmen, soon lined the streets of the business district. Lakeland was on its way.

The residents set about creating not just a collection of houses and businesses but a true community. Schools, churches, and hospitals were built. The town established parks and libraries. Using funds raised by public subscription, the Chautauqua Auditorium opened in 1912 as a venue for lectures, concerts, and other cultural programs. Civic clubs and social organizations proliferated. Municipal services including police and fire departments expanded. Several residents including Herbert Drane, Park Trammell, and Lawton Chiles rose to political prominence. Along the way to building a unified community, residents have also grappled with issues ranging from prohibition of alcohol to segregation.

In 1921, city officials convinced Southern College, an institution of higher learning later renamed Florida Southern College, to relocate to Lakeland. Dr. Ludd Spivey, the school's president, soon embarked on a course that would add a distinctive appearance to the campus. In 1938, Spivey asked one of the world's most innovative architects, Frank Lloyd Wright, to design "a great educational temple in Florida" to fit among the rolling hills of citrus groves. Listed on the National Register of Historic Places in 1975, the Florida Southern College Architectural District is known today as Frank Lloyd Wright's "Child of the Sun" collection, a name stemming from Wright's description of buildings that grew "out of the ground, into the light, a child of the sun."

Lakeland has also played a role in military history. The town felt the effects of war in 1898 as troops were temporarily quartered there during the Spanish-American War. Lakeland did its part during World War I and II, as residents served in both military and civilian capacities. During World War II, bond drives in Lakeland raised enough funds to purchase 15 additional bombers. Both fighter and bomber aircraft were stationed at Lakeland Army Air Field. The community also became home to more than 9,000 British and American flight cadets who trained at the Lodwick School of Aeronautics during the 1940s.

For many years Lakeland meant citrus to most people. During the 1980s, Lakeland and its surrounding area produced one-quarter of the nation's citrus. Although acreage is down, production has increased in recent years, with citrus still the most economically important crop in the county. Acres upon acres of strawberries and vegetables cover the ground outside of town, revealing the continuing importance of other agricultural products to the local economy. Phosphate first discovered in the late 1800s also has a major influence, as nearly three-quarters of the phosphate produced in the United States comes from within 25 miles of Lakeland. To avoid the potential downfalls of a narrowly based economy, today Lakeland actively promotes itself as a hub for product warehousing and distribution, service industries, and light manufacturing.

For those looking for a way to relax, Lakeland has plenty of answers. In 1926, the Lakeland Tourist Club listed on its rolls a total of 1,625 members from all over the world. In exchange for dues of just $1 per year, the organization offered ladies' afternoon parties and a Chautauqua series, as well as educational, literary, and musical programs. There were also dances, bridge, and euchre games, and theatre outings. Outdoor activities included motorcades, fishing, golf, miniature golf, tennis, horseshoes, and roque. Shuffleboard and lawn bowling were two activities whose popularity continued into the 1940s, 1950s, and 1960s. The sign at the Lakeland Lawn Bowling Club entrance advised participants, "Enjoy Yourself—It's Later Than You Think."

Today Lake Hollingsworth is home to the hydroplanes of the Orange Cup Regatta, while fishing, boating, and water sports of all kinds compete for the visitor's time. Lakeland also offers the chance to watch a major league baseball game, as the Detroit Tigers call Tigertown their own each year during spring training. Art shows such as Mayfaire-by-the-Lake attract thousands of art lovers each spring. Hundreds of thousands of would-be aviators dream of taking to the skies while watching thousands of airplanes during the annual Sun 'n Fun Fly-In, the second largest aviation event in the world. Just as its early promoters promised, Lakeland still offers something for everyone.

One
UNIQUELY LAKELAND

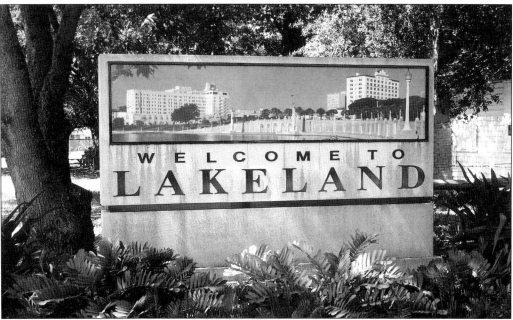

Situated along one of the roads leading into Lakeland today, this welcoming sign invites visitors to a community that is unique in many ways. For the history buff, Lakeland offers numerous examples of historic preservation, including the largest single-site collection of Frank Lloyd Wright's architecture in the world. For the artistically inclined, the city places a major emphasis on the performing and visual arts. Sports fans can cheer their favorite teams during spring training or take more active roles in water sports on the many lakes. Would-be aviators dream of taking to the skies while watching thousands of airplanes during the annual Sun 'n Fun Fly-In. Still a major citrus producer, the community is also surrounded today by acres and acres of ripe red strawberries each spring. Lakeland truly offers something for everyone. (Authors' Collection.)

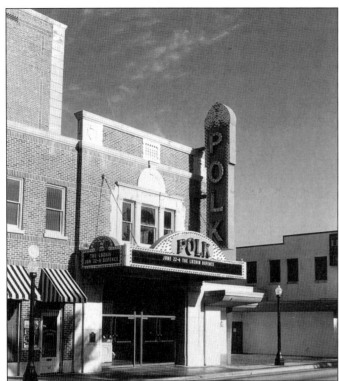

Unlike many communities that totally succumbed to the wholesale demolition that accompanied the urban renewal of the 1960s, Lakeland still retains many of its finest examples of early architecture. However, this has not happened by accident. Projects such as the restoration of the late 1920s Italian Renaissance-style Polk Theatre reflect the devoted efforts of preservation groups, city agencies, interested individuals, and a combination of private, state, local, and corporate funding. (Authors' Collection.)

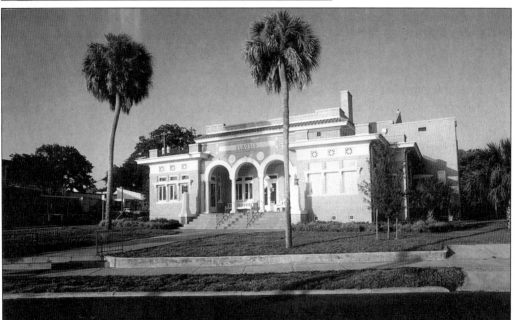

Founded in 1922, the Sorosis Club defined itself as "being sympathetic with, but in organization and concrete aims, independent of the Woman's Club, although a number of active workers are members of both organizations." Overlooking Lake Morton, the club's beautifully maintained yellow-brick building presently serves as the Lake Morton Senior Center and provides an excellent example of the adaptive reuse of historic structures. (Authors' Collection.)

Located at 230 South Florida Avenue, the Oates Building was built by Alvah Y. Oates during Florida's boom era to house the Oates Corley Furniture Company. Designed by noted architect Edward Columbus Hosford, the Mediterranean Revival-style building was later home to Maas Brothers Department Store. Following a $2 million restoration in 1994, the Oates Building was listed on the National Register of Historic Places. (Authors' Collection.)

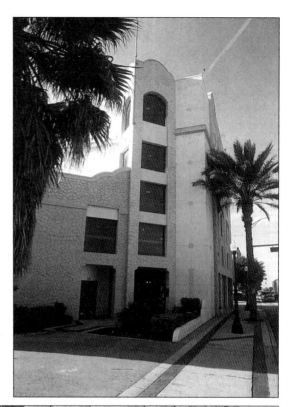

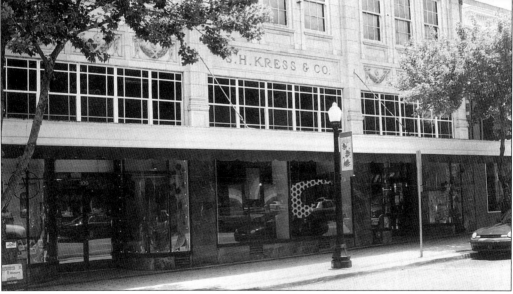

For many years, the stores of S.H. Kress & Company dotted the American landscape, selling a variety of low-priced merchandise and offering competition for the Woolworth and McCrory chains. The Kress properties were often very elaborate structures, many of which have since been demolished. Fortunately, Lakeland's Renaissance Revival-style Kress Building has been preserved and is home today to Explorations V Children's Museum, a "hands-on, fun-filled adventure in learning." (Authors' Collection.)

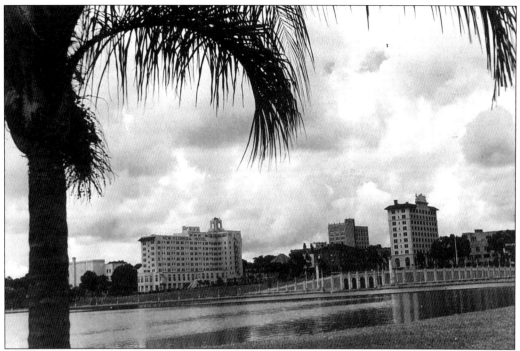

This image of the Lakeland skyline as viewed from Lake Mirror shows three of the tallest downtown buildings—the New Florida Hotel, the Marble Arcade, and the Hotel Terrace. It also shows the ongoing role of preservation groups such as Historic Lakeland, Inc. Two of the structures—the Marble Arcade and the Hotel Terrace—represent preservation victories. The fate of the New Florida remains a question mark. (Lakeland Public Library.)

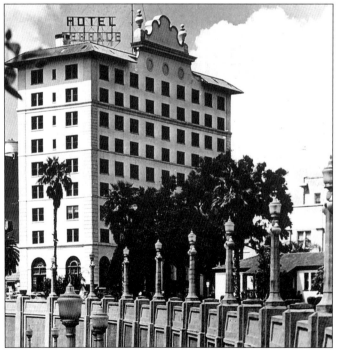

Opening in 1924 as the Hotel Lakeland Terrace, the 10-story, steam-heated, fireproof, 150-room structure was described as "The Top of Florida." Forty years later what had been "Florida's most modern hotel" had become weekly rentals, finally closing in 1986. Late in 1996, Mirror Properties Corporation and Marcobay Construction began work on the property, transforming it into the Terrace Hotel—a beautifully restored 88-room luxury hotel and a preservation victory. (Lakeland Public Library.)

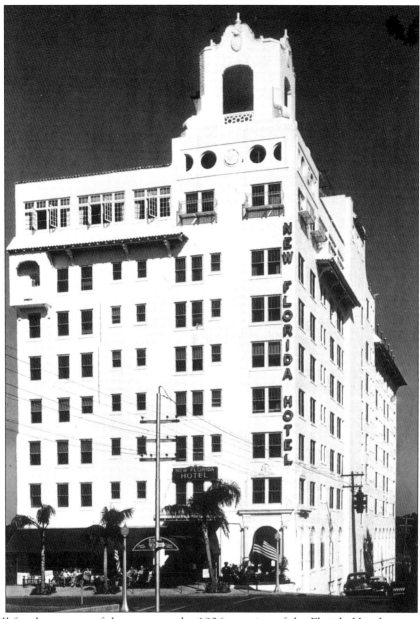

Boding ill for the success of the venture, the 1926 opening of the Florida Hotel occurred at the same time as the state's real estate boom ended. Reopening in 1936 as the New Florida Hotel, it bragged of being "Lakeland's largest and finest hotel—overlooking beautiful Lake Mirror and Civic Center." The impressive structure contained all of the elements of Spanish Revival-style architecture, including stuccoed walls, arched windows, a bell tower, decorative medallions, and a tile roof. That same year, radio station WLAK began broadcasting from a rooftop studio at the hotel. During World War II, civil defense observers stationed on the New Florida's roof scanned the skies for enemy planes. Converted in 1962 into a senior living center and later renamed the Regency Tower, the facility closed in 1996. While preservationists wage an ongoing battle for its restoration and propose alternative uses, others advocate the demolition of the city-owned New Florida Hotel. (Lakeland Public Library.)

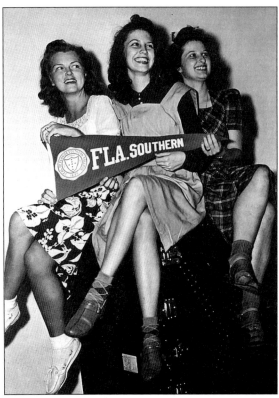

These coeds were students at Florida Southern College, one of the oldest private colleges in Florida and another "uniquely Lakeland" entity. Originally known as Southern College, the school had been located on Florida's West Coast near Palm Harbor. After a disastrous fire at the college in 1921, the City of Lakeland urged the school to relocate, donating a large tract of land on the north side of Lake Hollingsworth as a site for the campus. (Lakeland Public Library.)

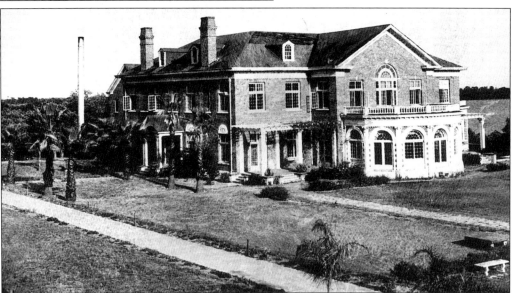

Lakeland officials also offered financial incentives to lure Southern College to their community. Although substantial and stately in appearance, the first two buildings, a dormitory for women and a combination dining hall/laboratory/classrooms/library, offered a very traditional appearance. Neither building at what would eventually become Florida Southern College gave any indication of the innovative architecture that would eventually bring national recognition to the institution. (Lakeland Public Library.)

Named president of Southern College in 1925, Dr. Ludd Spivey led the drive to dramatically increase enrollment and to expand the school's programs. Under his leadership, Florida Southern also embarked on a course that would add a distinctive appearance to the campus. One departure from the traditional was the acquisition of a Hindu temple. The temple and its accompanying statuary, a donation from Dr. Frederick B. Fisher, Methodist bishop of India, had been brought to the United States in the 1920s. Erected at Florida Southern in 1938, the Hindu Garden of Meditation added an ecumenical note to the campus design. (Lakeland Public Library.)

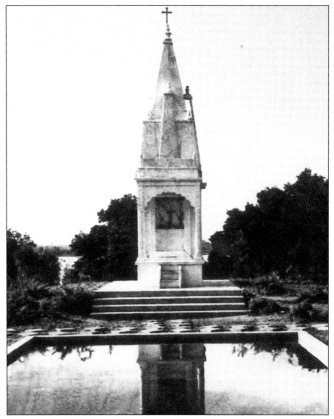

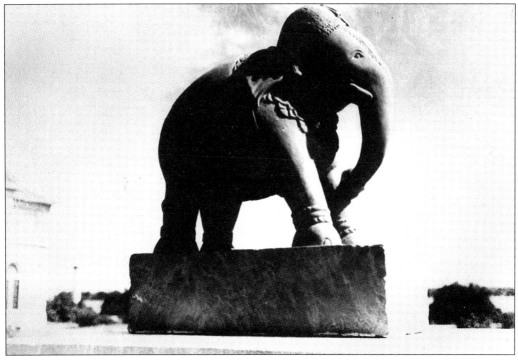

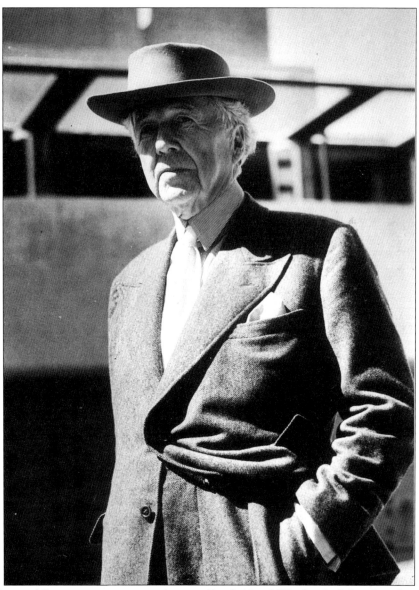

One of the world's most innovative architects, Frank Lloyd Wright, had developed an organic style of architecture that joined structures to the land, working with the environment rather than dominating it. In 1938, Florida Southern President Ludd Spivey asked the 67-year-old architect to design "a great educational temple in Florida" to fit among the rolling hills of citrus groves. Of the 18 structures designed, all were not constructed; nevertheless, those that were built comprise the largest single-site collection in the world of Wright's work. According to Wright's own description, the pattern of the West Campus was "the cultural value of organic buildings well suited to time, purpose, and place." Students performed much of the actual construction labor on several of the structures, working under Wright's personal supervision. The Annie Pfeiffer Chapel, incorporating all of the basic elements of his style, was the first of Wright's designs to be completed. The Polk County Science Building, containing the only Wright-designed planetarium to actually be constructed anywhere, was the last of his designs to be erected at Florida Southern. (Lakeland Public Library.)

Completed in 1968 at a cost of $1,278,960, the present E.T. Roux Library was designed not by Frank Lloyd Wright, but by Nils Schweizer, one of his students at Taliesin and the on-site supervisor for several of Wright's buildings at FSC. The 36,841-square-foot library, like the other Schweizer-designed buildings on campus, incorporates many of the elements favored by Frank Lloyd Wright in his work, however, and harmonizes beautifully with Wright's designs. (Authors' Collection.)

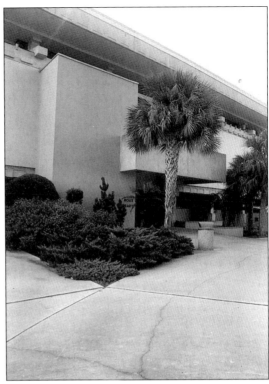

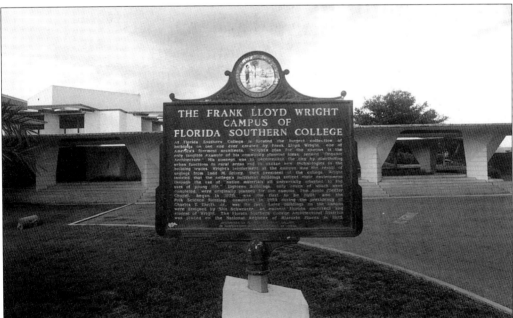

Listed on the National Register of Historic Places in 1975, the Florida Southern College Architectural District is known today as Frank Lloyd Wright's "Child of the Sun" collection, a name stemming from Wright's description of buildings that grew "out of the ground, into the light, a child of the sun." Using "native materials all universally adapted to the uses of young life," Wright created a unique educational environment. (Authors' Collection.)

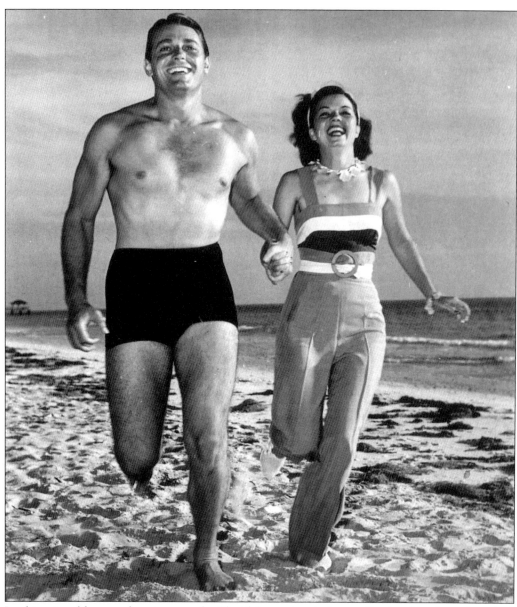
Looking just like an advertisement for Florida's tourism industry, Frances Newbern Langford and her husband Jon Hall were photographed running along a sandy beach. Rudy Valee reputedly discovered Langford during a Tampa radio program in 1931. A graduate of Lakeland High School and a Florida Southern College music major, she quickly gained fame as a popular radio performer and recording artist. Her Hollywood film career began in 1935 with a role in *Every Night at Eight*; even more popular than the movie, however, was her rendition of the film's song, "I'm in the Mood for Love." During World War II, Langford toured military bases both at home and abroad as part of Bob Hope's traveling USO show. She also entertained troops during the Korean Conflict and the war in Southeast Asia. Her film career spanned almost 20 years, culminating in 1954 with *The Glenn Miller Story*. Following her departure from Hollywood, Langford returned to Florida. She opened the Frances Langford Outrigger Resort in Jensen Beach where she continued to entertain fans until the mid-1980s. (Lakeland Public Library.)

Frances Langford's career as a performer included roles in nearly 30 movies, recordings of many popular songs, and appearances on numerous hit radio and television shows. The City of Lakeland formally recognized Langford's talents and accomplishments during a 1946 visit to her hometown, naming her as honorary mayor of the city and unveiling a marker proclaiming the Frances Langford Promenade along Lake Mirror. (Lakeland Public Library.)

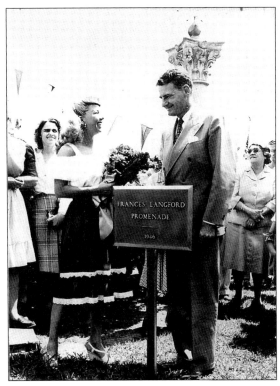

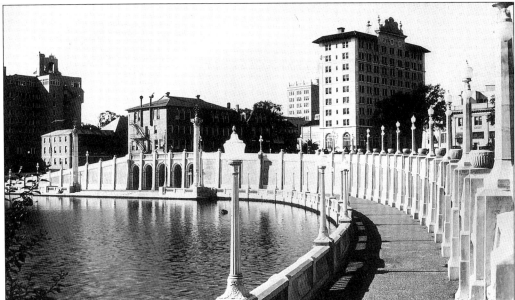

Taken from a vantage point looking toward the Terrace and New Florida hotels, this 1950s-era photograph shows the Lake Mirror Promenade, designed by noted landscape architect Charles Leavitt. Since its construction in 1928, Lakeland's residents and visitors alike have enjoyed strolling the ornately detailed walkway along the downtown lake. The restoration of the Lake Mirror Promenade to its original beauty was the first major project undertaken by Historic Lakeland, Inc. (Lakeland Public Library.)

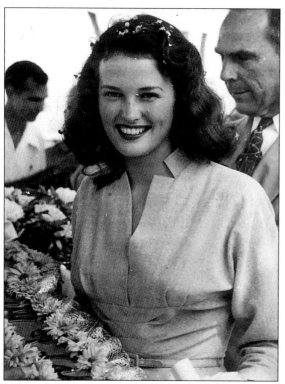

Frances Langford was not the only celebrity to come from Lakeland. More than 18,000 people in Atlantic City's Convention Hall watched as Neva Jane Langley was crowned as Miss America in 1953. The 19-year-old former Lakeland High School cheerleader bested a field of 52 contestants to win the coveted title. A student at Georgia's Wesleyan Conservatory and School of Fine Arts, she competed not as Miss Florida, however, but rather as Miss Georgia. (Lakeland Public Library.)

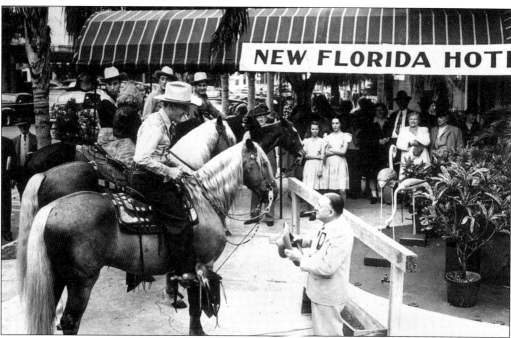

Lakeland has also had its share of famous visitors. In January 1947, spectators outside of the New Florida Hotel were treated to an appearance by popular cowboy film star and singer Jimmy Wakely, in town to participate in the Junior Chamber of Commerce rodeo. His newest movie, *Son of the Sierras*, opened at the Palace Theatre the following March. (Lakeland Public Library.)

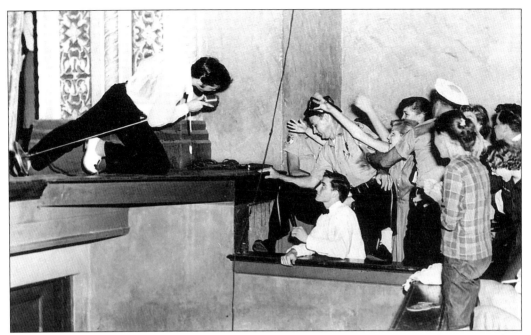

Less than 10 years later, the mere sight, let alone the sound, of Elvis Presley thrilled hundreds of screaming fans when Elvis appeared on the stage of Lakeland's Polk Theatre. His three performances on August 6, 1956, were part of a seven-city Florida tour that featured "The King" and his best-known songs, including "Hound Dog," "Heartbreak Hotel," and the ever-popular "Blue Suede Shoes." (Lakeland Public Library.)

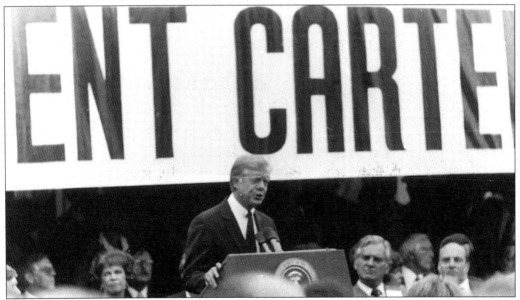

This audience appeared to be a bit more sedate than those attending the Elvis Presley concert pictured above. Nevertheless, these spectators still seemed to be paying close attention to the words of Jimmy Carter as he made a brief address during an appearance at Lakeland's Municipal Airport in 1980. Known as "the man from Plains, Georgia," Jimmy Carter served as president of the United States from 1977 until 1981. (Lakeland Public Library.)

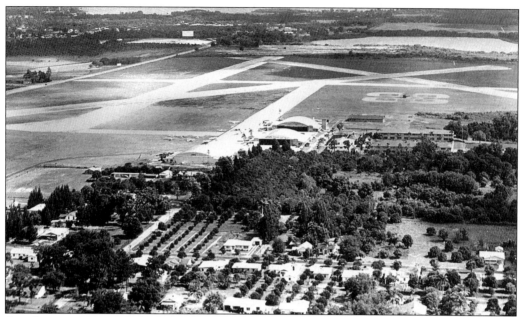

Another unique aspect of Lakeland is its aviation tradition. Although the area is known today as Tigertown, the official spring training home of the Detroit Tigers, this site originally served as the Lakeland Municipal Airport, a busy civil aviation scene from its inception. The airport took on a military focus in 1940 with the arrival of the Lodwick School of Aeronautics, which provided flight training for almost 9,000 British and American pilots during World War II. (Lakeland Public Library.)

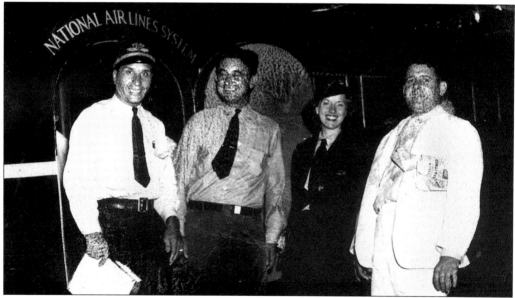

Commercial aviation had a place in Lakeland as well. When National Airlines began operation in St. Petersburg in 1934, stops in Tampa, Lakeland, and Daytona Beach were part of the initial route. Dick Bentley (second from left), Lakeland Municipal Airport's manager, was on hand to greet the arrival of the president of National Airlines, George Baker (fourth from left), and two members of the flight crew. (Lakeland Public Library.)

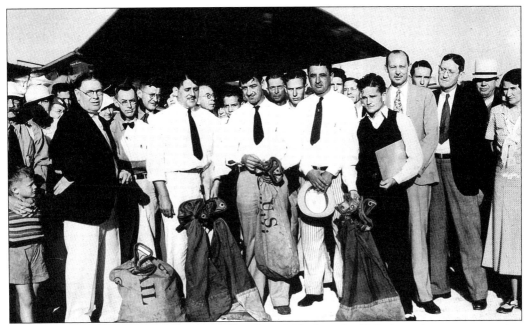

The delivery of mail by air had become official in 1918 when the U.S. Army began transporting mail; commercial airlines soon took over the task. It was not until October 15, 1934, that the first airmail flight into Lakeland took place, however. On that date, a crowd of spectators and dignitaries turned out to mark the momentous occasion. The gentleman dressed in a dark jacket and white pants and standing on the far left-hand side of the photograph was Lakeland's postmaster, Ferrell Smith. (Lakeland Public Library.)

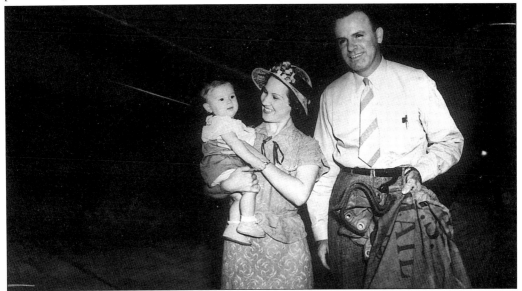

On May 19, 1938, in celebration of the 20th anniversary of airmail delivery, nine pilots from Central Florida converged on Lakeland's Municipal Airport with 184 pounds of specially postmarked bags of mail. Flying with Pete Sones, a Haines City pilot, were his wife Eleanor and infant son Peter Jr. Local newspapers touted the event with headlines that read, "Baby Sones Acts as Co-Pilot, Flying Air Mail with Father." (Lakeland Public Library.)

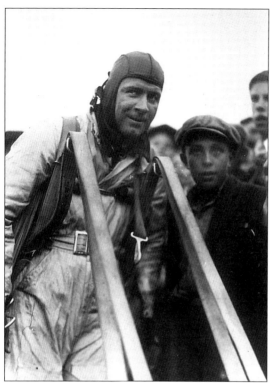

Frequently referred to as "The Golden Age of Aviation," the 1930s were filled with performances by daredevil aviators and barnstormers, air shows, and record-setting air races. Airports large and small provided venues for fliers to demonstrate their high-flying skills and stunts. Clem Sohn, known as the famous "Bat Man," appeared in Lakeland in January 1936. (Lakeland Public Library.)

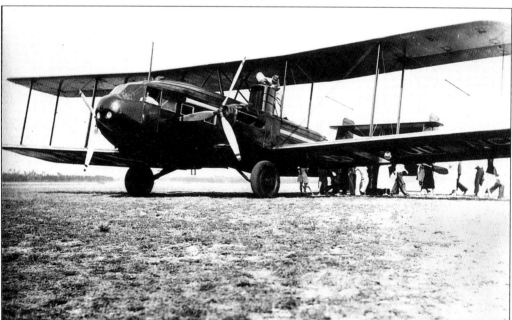

Another famous flier, Clarence D. Chamberlin, brought his huge 27-passenger Curtiss Condor to Lakeland as part of an extensive air tour of the United States in 1937. Local aviators George Haldeman and Ruth Elder had spent many hours in the skies above Lakeland 10 years earlier while training for their attempted crossing of the Atlantic Ocean in 1927. (Lakeland Public Library.)

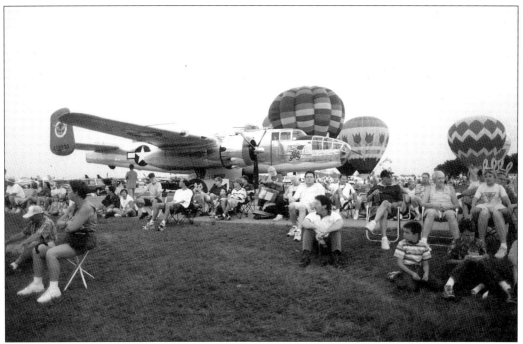

Lakeland is familiar to millions of people today as the home of the Sun 'n Fun EAA Fly-In, the second-largest aviation event in the world. In 1975, members of the Lakeland chapter of the Experimental Aircraft Association hosted a small weekend fly-in for aviation enthusiasts. From that modest beginning, the Fly-In today utilizes the Lakeland Linder Regional Airport to showcase a weeklong event that draws aircraft, aviators, exhibitors, and fans from all over the world. Attended by nearly 680,000 people, the 2000 Fly-In had an economic impact of almost $33 million. Wings 'n Things, a smaller event billed as a "Family Fun Fest," attracts additional visitors each fall. With a collection of more than 70 aircraft on display, the International Sport Aviation Museum (ISAM), located at the Sun 'n Fun complex on Medulla Road, offers a year-round opportunity to explore the world of aviation. (Sun 'n Fun Aviation Foundation.)

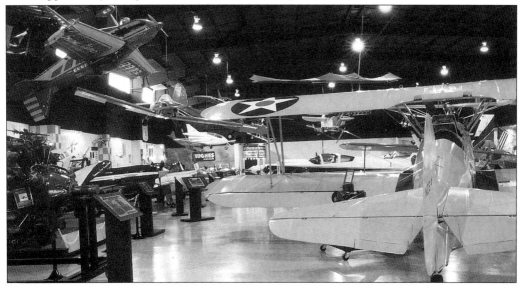

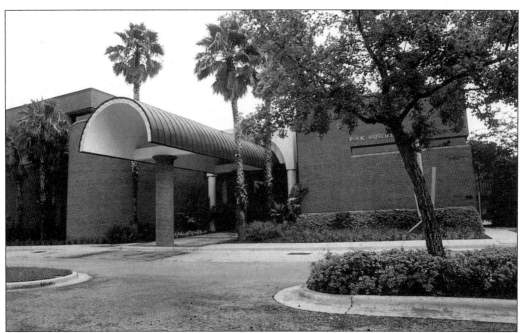

Another "uniquely Lakeland" element is the wealth of enriching opportunities for both visitors and residents by museums and other cultural organizations. Open free of charge to all visitors, the Polk Museum of Art is located near the shores of scenic Lake Morton, the site of the museum's annual outdoor art show, Mayfaire-by-the-Lake. Founded in 1966, the 37,000-square-foot museum includes nine galleries with both permanent and changing exhibitions. An outdoor sculpture garden offers additional enjoyment. Whether through educational programs, special events, or exhibits of European decorative arts, pre-Columbian, contemporary American, or Asian art, the Polk Museum of Art offers a variety of artistic experiences designed to fulfill its primary mission—introducing families to art. (Authors' Collection.)

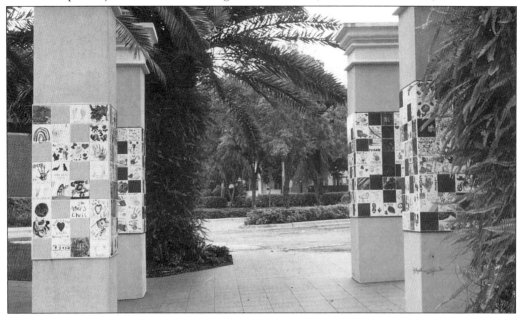

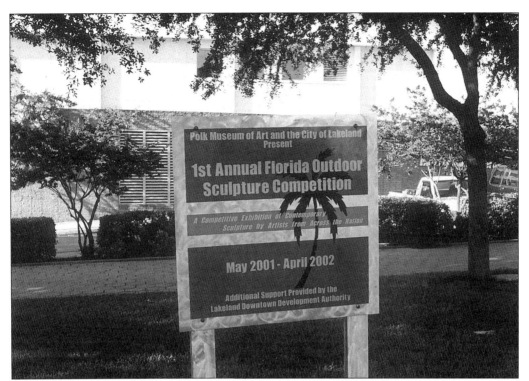

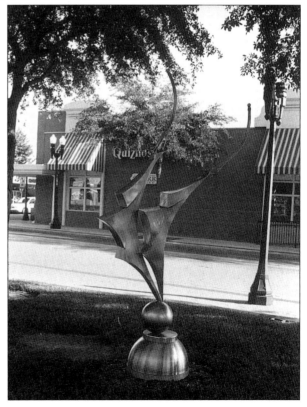

Other artistic opportunities also exist in Lakeland. Anyone strolling along the Lemon Street Promenade can absorb a bit of culture while enjoying the sunny weather. Presented by the Polk Museum of Art and the City of Lakeland, with additional corporate and community support, the First Annual Florida Outdoor Sculpture Competition officially opened on June 14, 2001. Ten outdoor sculptures selected for their aesthetic qualities and their ability to complement the outdoor setting were chosen from a field of 116 works by 51 artists. Among the more intriguing titles of the pieces are *Breaking New Ground*, *Clean-up*, *Southern Exposure*, and *Live Well!* The works of art will be displayed until April 2002. (Authors' Collection.)

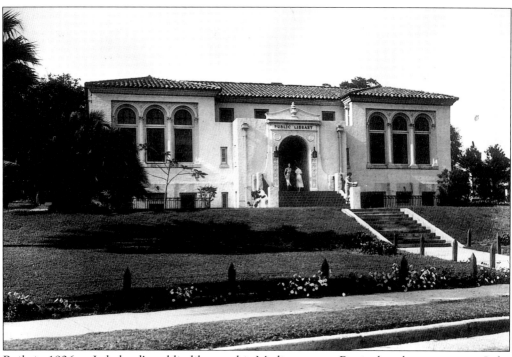

Built in 1926 as Lakeland's public library, this Mediterranean Revival–style structure on Lake Morton Drive was later named in honor of Park Trammell, former Lakeland mayor, Florida governor, and U.S. senator. As its collection grew, a new 35,674 square-foot library was built just across the lake. The present library at 100 Lake Morton Drive houses more than 167,000 volumes, 373 magazine titles, 19 newspapers, and 4,200 compact discs, as well as numerous archival collections. The Park Trammell Building is currently occupied by the Lakeland Chamber of Commerce. (Lakeland Public Library and Authors' Collection.)

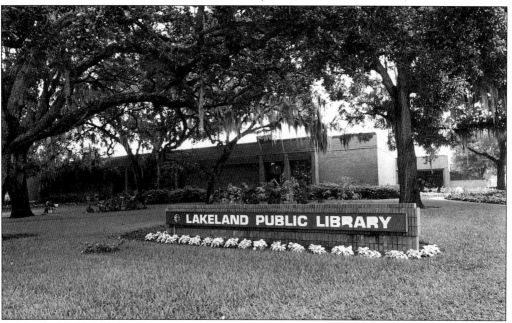

Two
PLACES AND FACES

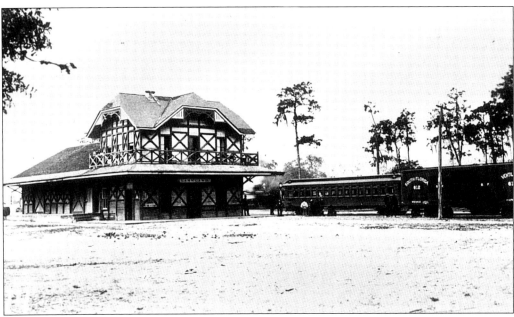

Communities develop as various events and individuals come together in a certain manner at a particular time and place. This was especially true in the case of Lakeland. While many Florida towns began when small groups of homesteaders banded together for protection or to pool resources, others were founded around the discovery of a particular natural resource in the area. Lakeland's birth and subsequent development were really linked to the coming of the railroad. As workers laid mile after mile of railroad track across Central Florida, small towns sprang up along the route. Land developers soon realized that the long-term viability of a community increased dramatically if the town was a regular stop for the railroad, as it delivered goods and passengers while transporting local products to markets. Lakeland's founder, Abraham Munn, insured the town's success in 1884 when he offered the railroad acreage for right-of-way and rail facilities, as well as a lavish $2,500 railroad station. (Lakeland Public Library.)

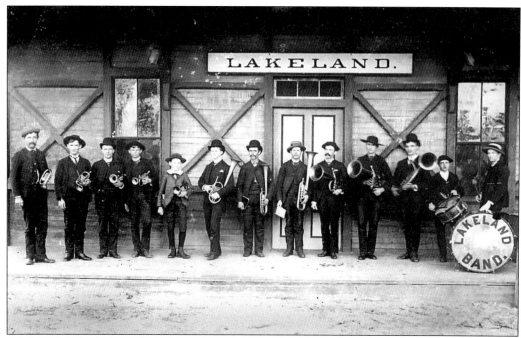

Everyone took part in a celebration of the arrival of the railroad in downtown Lakeland on October 15, 1885. By the mid-1890s, more than two dozen trains a day stopped at the Lakeland railroad station, bringing visitors on both a temporary and permanent basis. In 1895, Lakeland's very own brass band turned out to greet the arrival of a famous passenger—President Grover Cleveland. (Lakeland Public Library.)

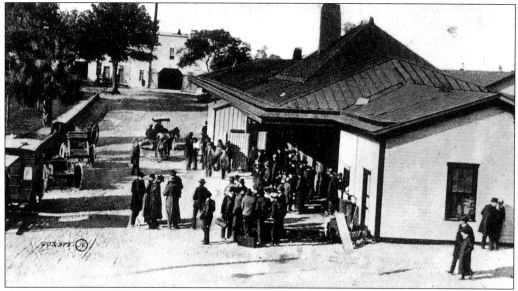

As rail transportation expanded, so did Lakeland. Unfortunately, rapid growth often resulted in hastily constructed wooden buildings that were easy prey for the many fires suffered by Florida cities in the late 1800s and early 1900s. Lakeland's railroad depots seemed especially vulnerable, with fires reported in 1893 and again in 1901. The extent of damage determined whether the depots were either completely or partially rebuilt. (Lakeland Public Library.)

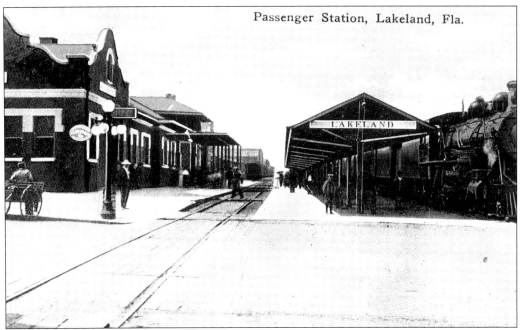

In 1910, the city sent W.K. Piner and M.F. Hetherington to Tallahassee to meet with the state railroad commission and representatives of the Atlantic Coast Line Railroad. Their task was to secure a new modern railroad station to replace the old one that was deemed to be inadequate. The men were successful—the new station opened with great fanfare as more than 1,000 people turned out to celebrate the occasion on March 14, 1912. (Lakeland Public Library.)

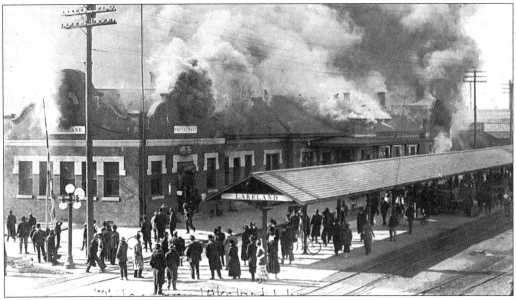

At the opening, Mayor S.L.A. Clonts voiced the pride that the community felt in its new station, calling it "a credit to a city many times larger." Unfortunately fire would strike again in February 1918, causing $25,000 in damage to the ACL station. Thanks to its brick construction, however, the damage could be repaired. The station, complete with the addition of a second floor, reopened on January 31, 1919. (Lakeland Public Library.)

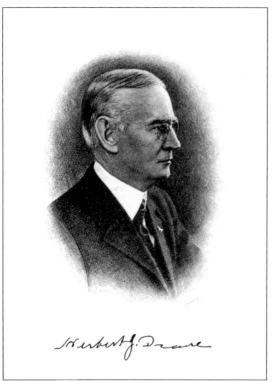

Beginning in 1883, Herbert J. Drane was inextricably linked with the growth of Lakeland. As construction supervisor of a section of the railroad from Kissimmee to Tampa, Drane set up a camp on Lake Wire, built the first drugstore in what would soon become Lakeland, and established the county's first insurance firm. Along with his varied business interests, Drane was active in civic life, serving as clerk, treasurer, and mayor of Lakeland, county commissioner, state representative, and state senator. He also represented Florida during multiple terms in the U.S. Congress. Reputedly the first house in Lakeland to have indoor plumbing, Drane's home was located in the midst of a 10-acre orange grove on West Hillcrest Drive. Demolished in 1948, the house had been enlarged from a four-room dwelling to a 15-room mansion during the more than 50 years of Drane's residence. (Lakeland Public Library.)

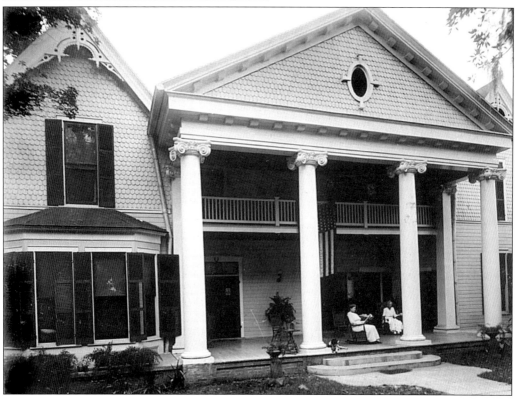

Abraham G. Munn, considered to be the founder of Lakeland, fell in love with Florida while on a visit from Kentucky in 1879. Three years later, he purchased several thousand acres of land in the central part of the state. He then instructed Samuel Munn, his son and a civil engineer, to plat a tract of 80 acres as the new town of Lakeland. Along with being responsible for bringing the railroad to Lakeland, Munn spearheaded much of the development in the area as head of the Lakeland Improvement Company. (Lakeland Public Library.)

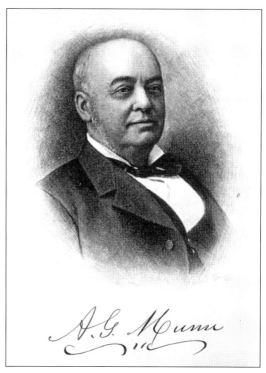

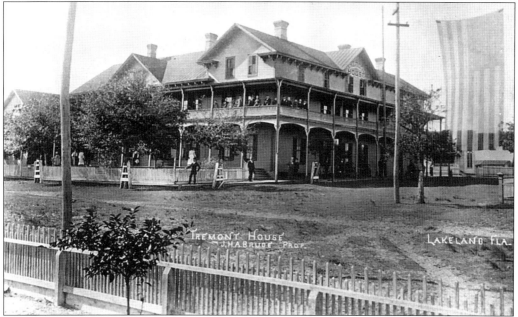

Realizing that rail transportation would bring travelers to Lakeland, Munn built Tremont House, the town's first hotel, at the corner of Main Street and Massachusetts Avenue in 1885. Costing $20,000 to construct and managed for many years by Col. J.H.A. Bruce, the hotel was once considered one of the most elegant in Central Florida. Advertisements claimed, "The Tremont Hotel is to Lakeland what the Waldorf-Astoria is to New York—a hotel par excellence." (Lakeland Public Library.)

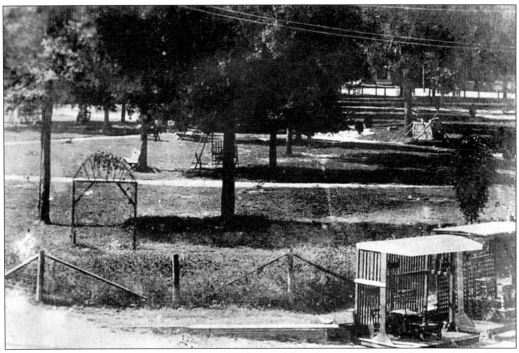

Abraham Munn's civic generosity extended beyond his donation of land for a railroad depot. He also contributed a square block of land in the center of the new town to be used as a city park. While Munn had refused to allow the community to be named Munnville in his honor several years earlier, he did accede to popular sentiment in one regard. With his approval, in April 1908 city council passed a resolution designating the grounds as Munn Park. (Lakeland Public Library.)

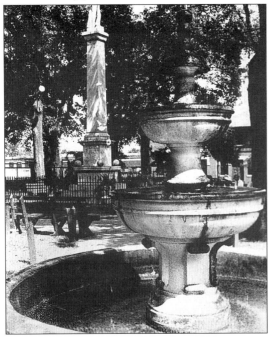

Confederate sympathies survived in Lakeland long after the Civil War. This 1936 photograph of Munn Park shows not only a fountain, but also a tall monument surrounded by an iron fence. Dedicated to the soldiers of the Confederacy, the statue of a soldier atop a marble pillar was unveiled on June 3, 1910, the birthday of Jefferson Davis. Nearly two years later, the Lakeland chapter of the United Daughters of the Confederacy finished paying for its $1,750 cost. (Lakeland Public Library.)

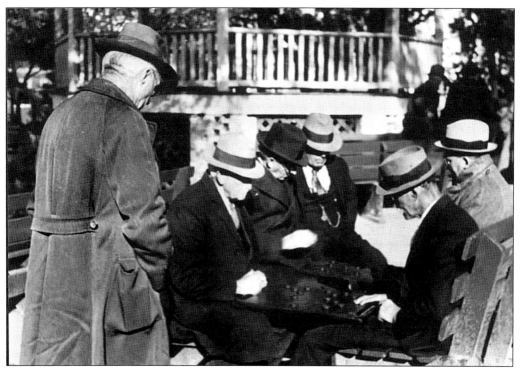

Munn Park has been a center of community activity since its inception. After a disastrous fire in 1904, the park held temporary business structures. In 1917, Lakeland's citizens came to Munn Park to listen to a speech by Teddy Roosevelt. Band concerts took place in the park. The founder and editor of the *Lakeland Ledger and Star-Telegram*, Sam Farabee (center, wearing black hat), met other gentlemen at the park for games of checkers, while still other local residents came to the park just to relax or to feed the birds. (Lakeland Public Library.)

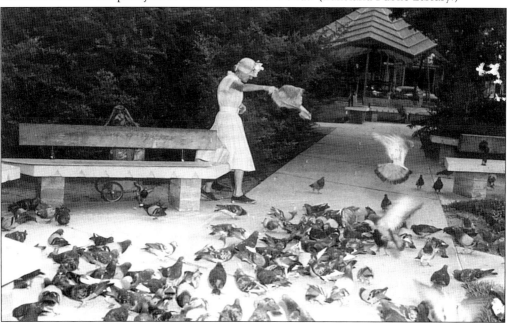

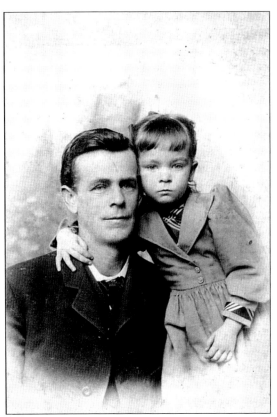

The Riggins family played an important role in Lakeland's early history. The patriarch of the family, M.P. Riggins, came to Lakeland in 1884, becoming one of the town's first merchants. After his death in 1895, M.P. Riggins's son Norman took over the family enterprises that included a retail store, commercial farmland, and a sawmill along the shores of Lake Morton. He eventually relocated the mill closer to the railroad on Florida Avenue. The lumber mill formed the nucleus of a business empire that included a rice mill, icehouse, and novelty works. In addition to his varied commercial interests, Norman Riggins also played an active role in civic affairs, serving as a member of the school board, city council member, and bond trustee. In 1893 Norman Riggins posed for this photograph with his daughter Fannie. (Lakeland Public Library.)

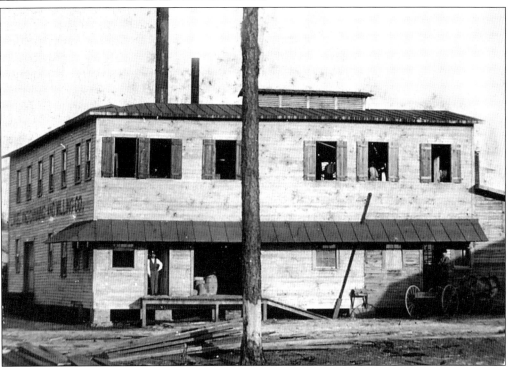

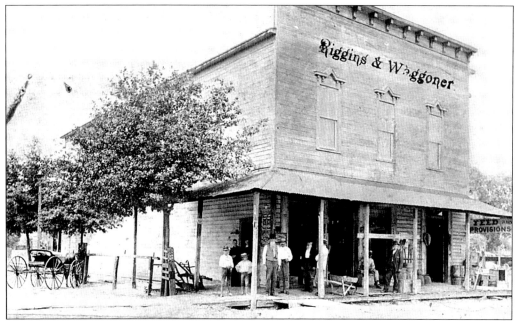

The Riggins & Waggoner store at the corner of Main Street and Tennessee Avenue was one of the earliest of the family's enterprises. Founded by M.P. Riggins and C.W. Waggoner in 1884, the store carried an assortment of merchandise, from groceries and household goods to clothing and hardware items. The equivalent of modern department stores, the Riggins & Waggoner emporium provided many necessities for Lakeland's residents. (Lakeland Public Library.)

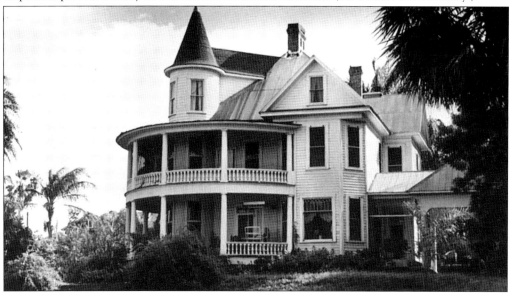

Situated on six acres overlooking Lake Morton, Norman Riggins's home contained ten rooms and three baths. Photographed for a souvenir edition of the *Lakeland News* in 1905, Mosswood was one of Lakeland's most impressive residences. Along with the moss-draped trees that gave the house its name, royal palms reputedly brought from Thomas Edison's residence in Fort Myers enhanced the landscaping. Moved across the street in 1952, the Victorian-style dwelling survives today as a Lakeland landmark. (Lakeland Public Library.)

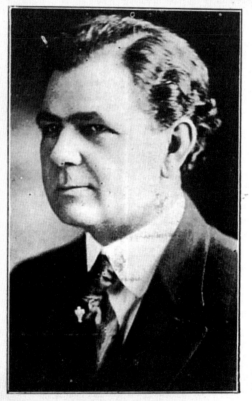

While Lawton M. Chiles, Florida's 41st governor, was the most recent Lakeland resident to achieve national political prominence, Park Trammell was one of the first. Following his graduation from law school, Trammell opened a legal practice in Lakeland in 1899. Elected mayor that same year, he represented Polk County in the state legislature in 1902 and became state senator in 1905. Four years later, Trammell became Florida's attorney general, and in 1913, was elected as the 21st governor of the state. Before his tenure as governor ended, he was elected to the first of multiple terms as a U.S. senator. This piece of campaign literature touts the many accomplishments that contributed to Park Trammell's successful political career. (Lakeland Public Library.)

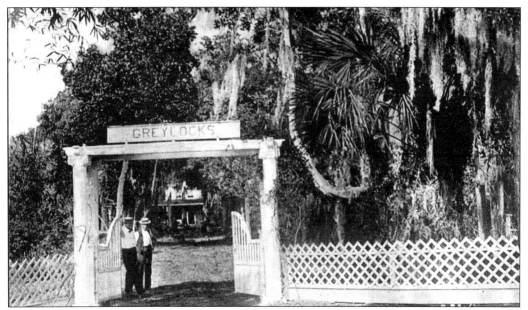

Senator Park Trammell and his wife Beatrice bought the property known as Greylocks in 1928, residing there until his death eight years later. At the time, the residence already had a long history as a Lakeland showplace. One of the most elegant dwellings in town, the home was the scene of many social events over the years, including Florida Southern College receptions and dances. The original owner was S.M. Stephens, a major citrus shipper, who built Greylocks on an 8.5-acre site along the shore of Lake Hollingsworth in 1885. As part of an extensive remodeling in 1919, a two-story colonnaded facade was added. Following the death of James Raulerson, the last owner, the once-beautiful dwelling stood vacant and vandalized. Severely damaged by fire in 1965, Greylocks was demolished two years later. (Lakeland Public Library.)

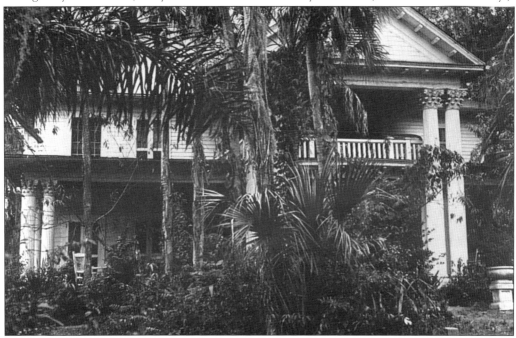

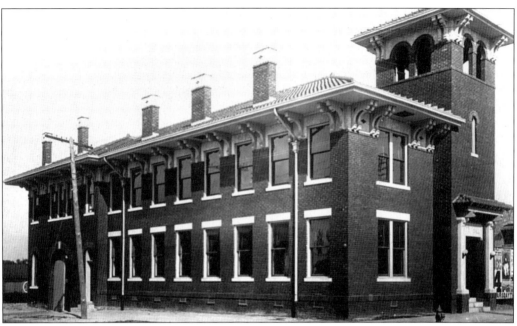

Civic institutions also played an important role in the development of the community. City hall took on a more Mediterranean look when Lakeland residents erected an Italian Villa–style structure in 1913 to house city offices, the fire department, and jail. Located at 100 East Main Street, the building served as the center of municipal government until a new city hall was constructed during the 1920s on South Massachusetts Avenue. (Lakeland Public Library.)

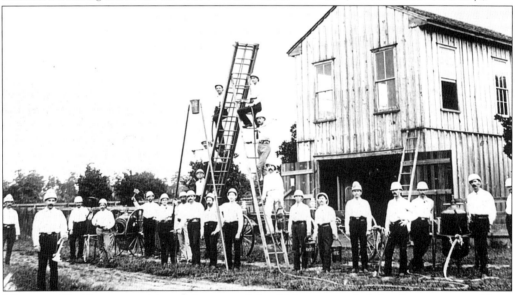

Like most Florida communities at the turn of the 20th century, Lakeland was protected from fire by the diligent efforts of private citizens who turned out in response to the cry of "Fire!" In 1891, total firefighting equipment consisted of two dozen buckets, two axes, and two ladders. Finally in 1909, a volunteer department under the leadership of Chief H.L. Swatts was organized. Not until the fire department moved into the new city hall did it acquire its first piece of motorized equipment. (Lakeland Public Library.)

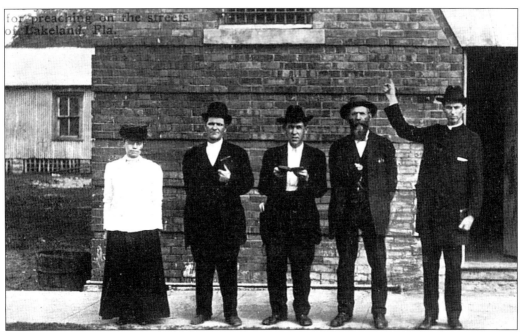

In its earliest days, Lakeland's jail (also referred to as a calaboose) was known as McDermott House, supposedly named for its first inhabitant. A photograph dated November 11, 1912, pictured the jail and five of its residents—incarcerated for the crime of preaching on the streets of Lakeland. By the following year, the jail had relocated to the new city hall. Over the ensuing years, a succession of different buildings would serve as headquarters for the police department and the jail. (Lakeland Public Library.)

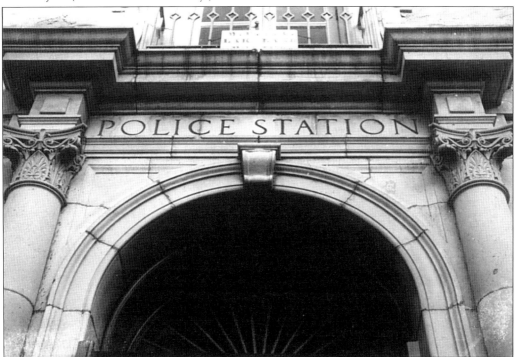

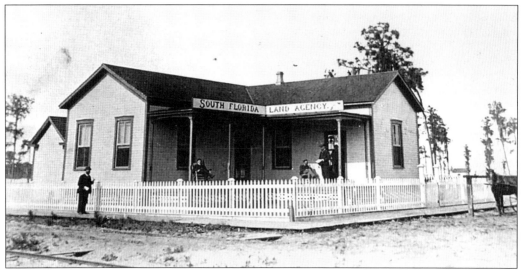

"If you want a good investment or a home in the 'Bright Sunny South,' tell it to us." "Openings for good investments and business enterprises for parties looking for same." With those and similar advertisements, real estate firms did all that they could to convince potential investors that Lakeland was the perfect place to own property. Calling the community "The Garden Spot of the South," companies like the South Florida Land Agency advocated Lakeland's growth almost from its inception. (Lakeland Public Library.)

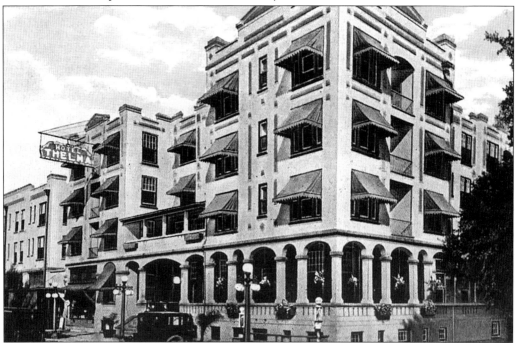

A believer in that potential growth, H.B. Carter came to Lakeland in 1901 from North Carolina and immediately began buying thousands of acres of undeveloped land as well as existing buildings and businesses. In 1919, Carter purchased the Hotel Kibler, built for $125,000 just six years earlier, and promptly renamed it the Hotel Thelma in honor of his daughter. (Lakeland Public Library.)

As more and more people believed in the state's potential, the land boom took off in the early 1920s. Real estate sales—and likewise prices—soared. In an effort to prove that bigger is truly better, the ten-story Marble Arcade on the northwest corner of Lemon Street was built in 1926. Newspaper accounts touted E.J. Spark's new high-rise, being constructed by George A. Miller of Tampa at a cost of $370,000, as Lakeland's tallest and finest office building. (Lakeland Public Library.)

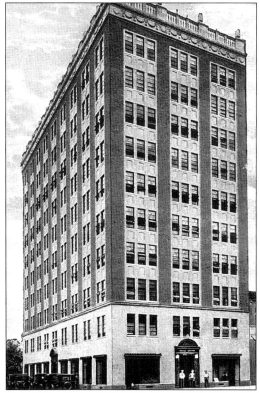

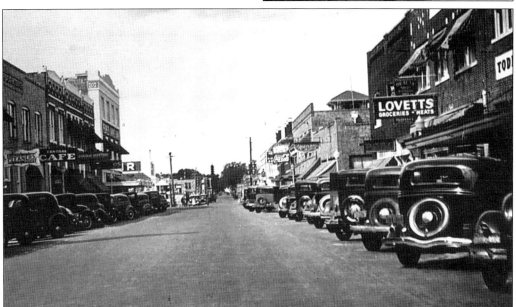

The boom was not to last, however. By 1927, as the bottom fell out of the real estate market, Lakeland, and indeed all of Florida, began to experience an economic depression that wouldn't hit Wall Street for several more years to come. Although Florida Avenue appeared busy in this 1936 street scene, Lakeland's residents were in the same dire financial straits as the rest of the country. (Lakeland Public Library.)

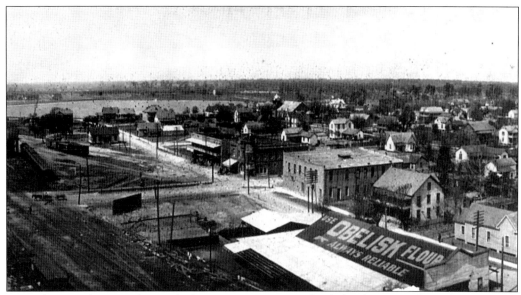

An unknown photographer took this panoramic view of Lakeland in 1905 from the old water tank at the corner of Massachusetts and Rose. It revealed a steadily growing Central Florida town with its residential area spreading out beyond a small business district. A horse-drawn wagon was making its way down dusty, dirt streets toward the all-important railroad lines. Much of the land in the background appears to be vacant. (Lakeland Public Library.)

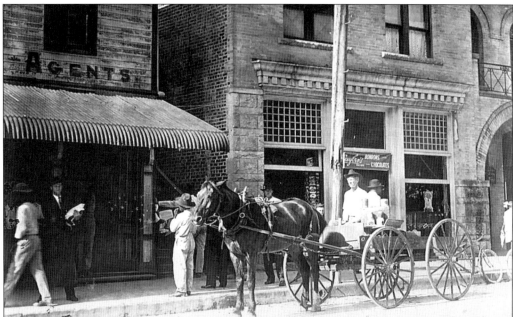

Details of Lakeland's growth could be seen in this photograph taken just three years later. Workmen in overalls stand beside businessmen dressed in coats and ties. Adjacent to the wooden structure with the "Agents" sign visible above the entrance is the Kentucky Building, built in 1903 and the first masonry building south of the railroad. Along with other businesses, the Italianate style structure housed a store selling bonbons and chocolates on the first floor and the offices of Dr. W.R. Groover on the second. (Lakeland Public Library.)

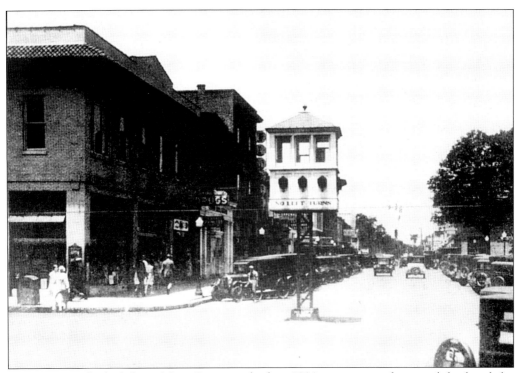

As the viewer looked down Main Street in the late 1920s, two rows of automobiles lined the now-paved streets while still more cars searched for parking places. Epitomizing the growth of the community, a traffic light tower had recently been installed at the intersection of Main Street and Kentucky Avenue. With perhaps the exception of the most ardent of real estate promoters, however, few residents at that time envisioned the development that would occur during the approximately 40 years that separated these two images. (Lakeland Public Library.)

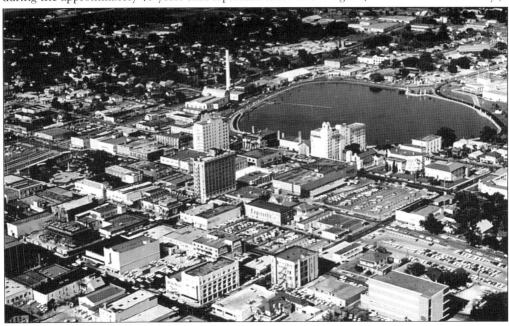

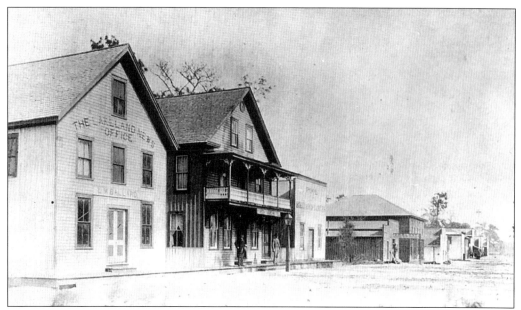

The *Lakeland News* claimed the distinction of being the community's first newspaper with the premiere issue printed on June 10, 1884. Publisher L.M. Ballard operated a general store on the first floor of a building at the corner of Florida Avenue and Pine Street; the newspaper offices were located on the second floor. Under different owners, the name of the newspaper would change repeatedly, becoming *The Florida Cracker*, the *Lake Region Sun*, and eventually the *Lakeland Sun*. (Lakeland Public Library.)

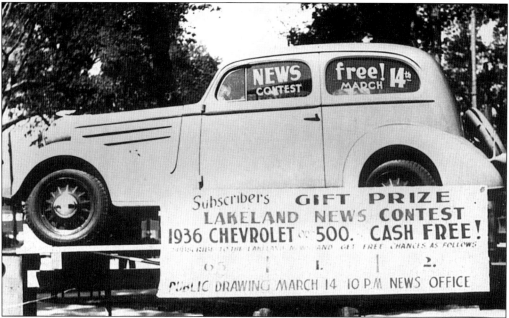

With nothing but the name to connect it to the city's original paper, the *Lakeland News* would reappear in 1900. By 1905, the paper was operating from the Kentucky Building and offering a yearly subscription for just $1. Thirty years later, the *Lakeland News* was waging a battle for new subscribers with the promise of free raffle tickets for a new car. (Lakeland Public Library.)

A town's newspapers both reflect and shape the character of the community. Lakeland was certainly no exception with several newspapers competing for the literary attention of local residents. In 1905, M.F. Hetherington, right, the former publisher of the Miami daily paper, purchased the *Lakeland News*. Two years later he bought out his major competition, the *Lakeland Sun*, consolidating the two papers. In 1911, Hetherington expanded his journalistic domain with the founding of the *Lakeland Evening Telegram*, the town's first daily paper. So successful was the enterprise that it moved into its own building in 1913. Sold in 1920, the *Evening Telegram* merged with the local morning paper two years later to form the *Star-Telegram*. M.F. Hetherington also utilized his extensive knowledge to author his *History of Polk County*, a volume considered for many years to be the definitive account of the region. (Lakeland Public Library.)

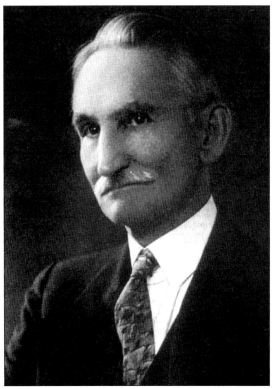

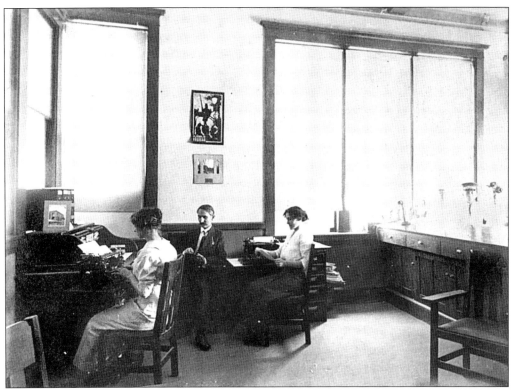

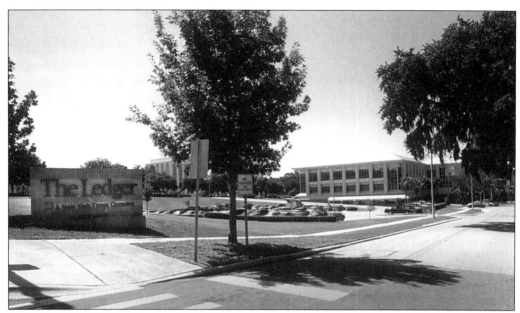

With Sam Farabee as editor and Earl Mullen as business manager, the *Lakeland Evening Ledger* began publication in September 1924. Following a merger with the *Star-Telegram* in 1928, it became known as the *Lakeland Evening Ledger and Star-Telegram*. Operating today from a $72-million facility constructed in 1998 and owned by the *New York Times* Company, the *Ledger* continues to serve as Lakeland's major newspaper. (Lakeland Public Library.)

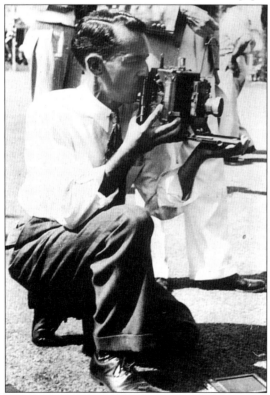

More than 6,000 negatives of photographs taken by Dan Sanborn during his journalistic career are housed in the Special Collections unit of the Lakeland Public Library. Shown with his ever-present camera, Sanborn worked for the *Lakeland Evening Ledger and Star-Telegram* during the 1930s, for the Lodwick School of Aeronautics in 1941, and as a self-employed photographer following World War II. His photographic documentation of local events remains a treasure trove for any researcher. (Lakeland Public Library.)

Three
THE FABRIC OF SOCIETY

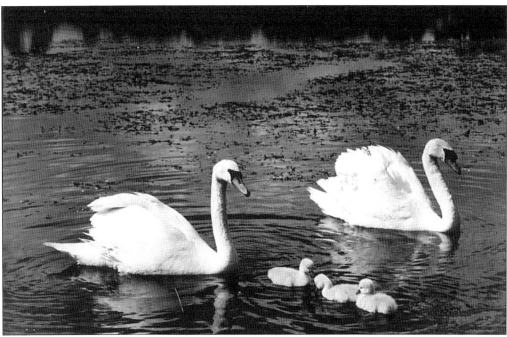

These swans and their cygnets swimming on Lake Morton are more than just a bucolic scene. A symbol of what Lakeland has become, representations of swans appear everywhere in town—in store windows, on library counters, on promotional literature, and on banners hanging from streetlights. Replacing a globe that depicted Lakeland as the citrus center of the world, the new logo offers another view of the way in which residents see themselves and their thriving, multi-faceted community. Historian Will Durant wrote, "Civilization is like a stream with banks. People build homes, love, raise children, sing songs, write poetry, and even whittle statues. The story of civilization is the story of what happened on the banks." Still others would describe a community's actions and institutions as the fabric of society. (Lakeland Public Library.)

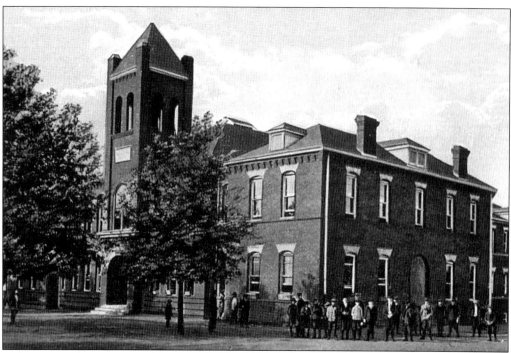

One of the most important actions taken by the residents of any community, however large or small, is to provide the best possible schools for their children. With its description of the town's recently built high school, the *Lakeland News* in 1905 gave voice to residents' pride. "There are few finer school buildings in the state than the Lakeland High School—certainly there is none superior in any town of the same size. This building was recently finished at a cost of $10,000, and is an architectural gem." The first class to graduate from the new school consisted of just four students—three girls and one boy. The school also fielded a football team, with its members proudly posing for this group photo. Less than 20 years later, Lakeland High School's Dreadnoughts won the 1923 state football championship. (Lakeland Public Library.)

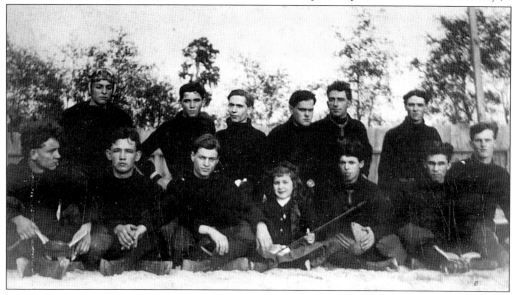

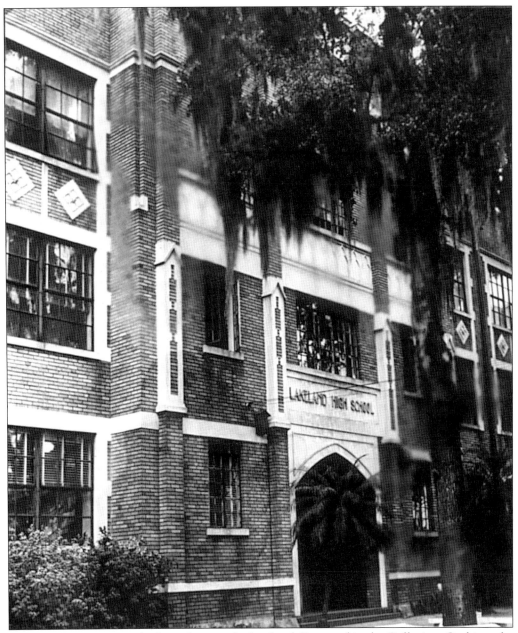

By 1927, the community had another new high school. Designed in the Collegiate Gothic style, the H-shaped, three-story, 54,000-square-foot building provided the setting for the education of thousands of Lakeland's residents. After being abandoned for several years, the building was renovated in 1995 as the Lakeland Middle Academy, a magnet school for approximately 600 pupils. In 1999, it was renamed as Lawton Chiles Middle Academy in honor of the former governor. Along with Spessard Holland and several other well-known Floridians, Chiles was an alumnus of Lakeland High School. In recognition of the significance of its location, design, materials, and workmanship, the building was listed on the National Register of Historic Places in 1993. Several other Lakeland schools have also received landmark status for their architectural and historical significance. (Lakeland Public Library.)

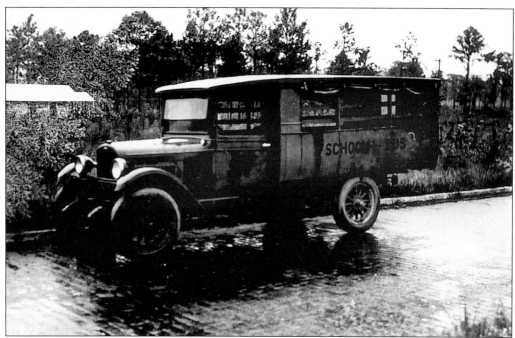

Not all of the pupils attending classes in Lakeland lived within walking distance of the school. For those students who lived in outlying areas, the school board provided bus transportation. While these buses were not necessarily state-of-the-art conveyances, students were fortunate to be provided with any transportation at all, since beginning teachers with a four-year degree earned only $720 per year in wages. (Lakeland Public Library.)

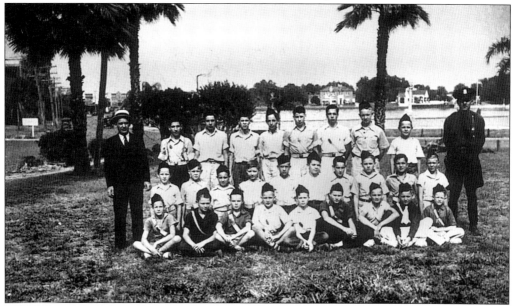

Athletics were not the only extracurricular activities for students attending Lakeland's schools. These young, pictured on May 11, 1938, are the members of the school safety patrol. Pictured with them are Police Chief Roy Hutchingson and Officer Leo Brooker. Hutchingson served as Lakeland's chief of police from 1933 until 1951. (Lakeland Public Library.)

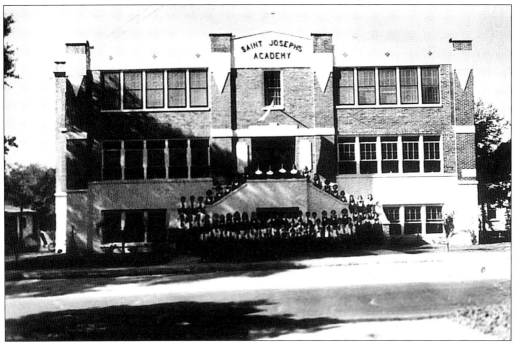

Lakeland acquired a parochial school when the former Polk County Works Progress Administration office was donated to Saint Joseph's parish. Originally built as Morrell Memorial Hospital in 1916, the structure at 223 South Missouri Avenue opened as Saint Joseph's Academy in 1939. With the girls dressed in dark jumpers with white blouses and the boys wearing dark pants, white shirts, and neckties, the pupils epitomized correct attire and decorum as they learned their lessons under the supervision of the Sisters of Saint Joseph. (Lakeland Public Library.)

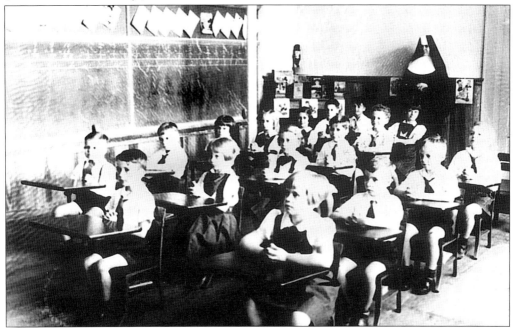

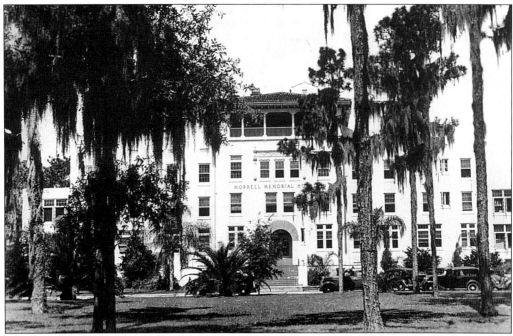

Thanks to a bequest of land from Mrs. F.A. Morrell and a $15,000 bond issue approved by the citizenry, Lakeland acquired a hospital in 1916. With 65 beds and a staff of 24, Morrell Memorial Hospital cared for the medical needs of local residents until a larger, more modern facility was built in 1926. From these roots has grown the Lakeland Regional Medical Center, one of Florida's largest hospitals with nearly 900 beds. (Lakeland Public Library.)

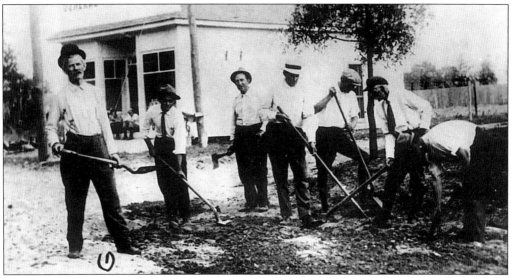

Building a community required cooperation from everyone. Whether civic endeavors or special projects, people worked together to achieve common goals. In this particular instance, members of the Dixieland Methodist Church pooled their skills to build a new church. Beginning at sunrise, the men worked on the construction, while the women of the congregation brought nourishing meals to the site throughout the day. The new church building was completed in time for services that evening. (Lakeland Public Library.)

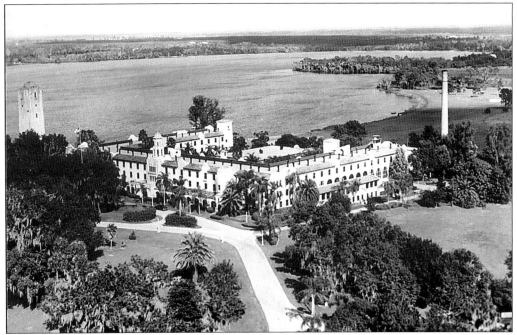

Almost 2,000 acres of land along Lake Gibson bustled with activity in the late 1920s as the United Brotherhood of Carpenters and Joiners of America spent more than $1 million to construct a retirement home. Dedicated on October 2, 1928, the Carpenters and Joiners Home included rooms for as many as 400 residents, a laundry, power plant, and water tower, surrounded by landscaped grounds and citrus groves. Finally closing in 1976, it was purchased by the First Assembly of God Church four years later. The congregation then constructed a new church building on the grounds, while renovating the original structure as a school. The Carpenters Home, with its ornate architecture and impressive arched entrance, was listed on the National Register of Historic Places in 1990. (Lakeland Public Library.)

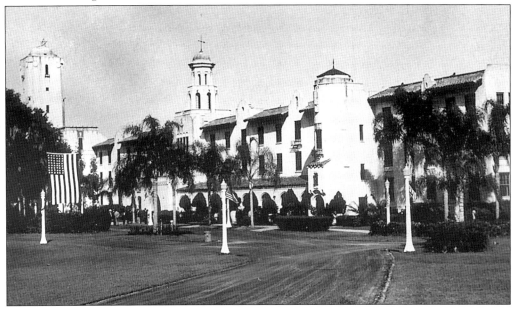

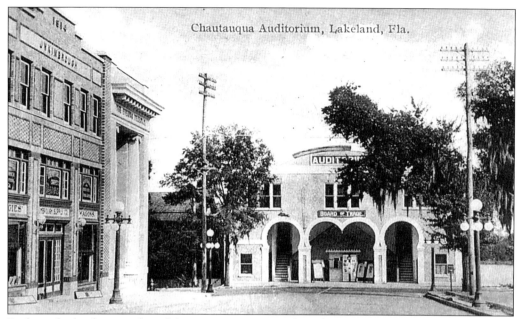

Built with funds contributed by private citizens, the Chautauqua Auditorium opened on November 6, 1912, with a theatrical performance followed by an address by Herbert Drane, Florida state senator. Standing at the east end of Main Street overlooking Lake Mirror, the 1,700-seat auditorium was reputedly one of the largest in the state. William Jennings Bryan, famed orator and frequent Democratic presidential candidate, often lectured at Lakeland's Chautauqua Auditorium. (Lakeland Public Library.)

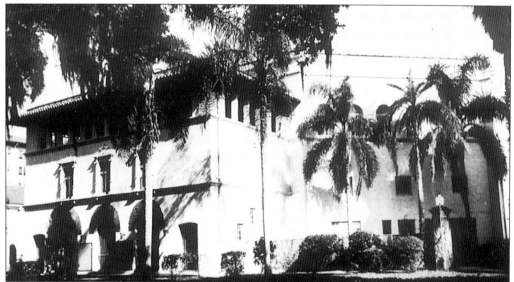

A bond issue in June 1924 authorized an expenditure of $100,000 for the site and $300,000 for the construction of a new city hall and an adjacent municipal auditorium. Replacing the old Chautauqua Auditorium, the new facility seated 1,500 people for lectures, plays, concerts, and other performances. From the early 1940s until its demolition in 1969, City Auditorium was called Mayhall Auditorium in honor of Harry Mayhall, Lakeland High School's music director. (Lakeland Public Library.)

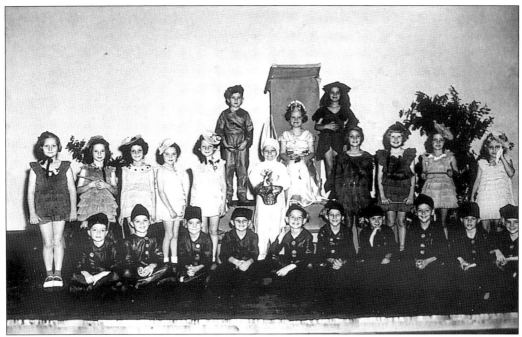

As one more thread in the fabric of society, public performances offer local residents an opportunity to showcase their particular talents and attributes. Whatever their age, eventual occupation, and place in society, adults still remember the time when they appeared in their school play as reigning royalty, a white rabbit, a flower, or other cast member. And regardless of the eventual winner, any woman who ever competed in a beauty pageant remembers her moment in the limelight. These second-graders starred in *The First Easter Egg* at Lake Morton School in 1938, while the beauty pageant on July 2, 1941, culminated in the selection of Ivie Anne Hall as Miss Lakeland. (Lakeland Public Library.)

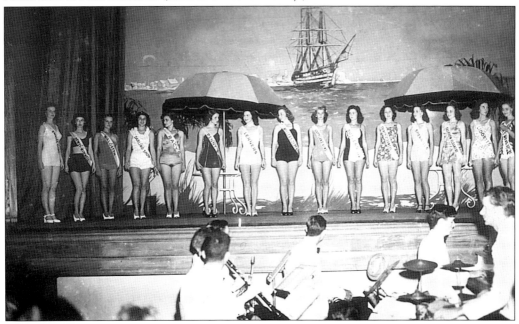

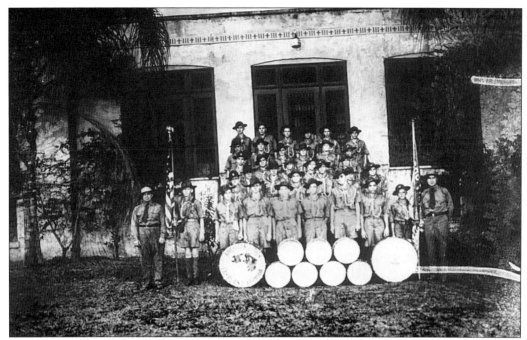

Social service organizations also play an important role in community life. The Lakeland troop of the Boy Scouts of America had its beginnings in the office of Judge Kelsey Blanton on June 4, 1913. Twenty-five years later, the Boy Scout drum and bugle corps won first prize in the state competition at the American Legion convention in Jacksonville. (Lakeland Public Library.)

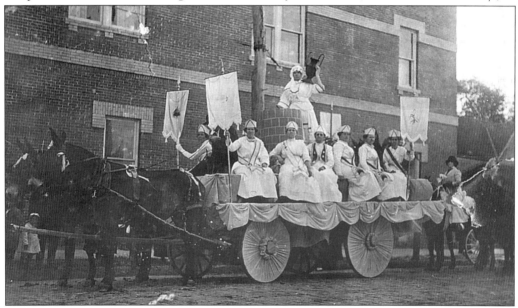

Lakeland also had its share of organizations for adults. The United Confederate Veterans, Benevolent Order of Elks, Odd Fellows Lodge, Knights of Pythias, American Legion, Exchange, Kiwanis, and Rotary clubs were just a few of the organizations for men. The ladies of the community had their own organizations, including the Daughters of the Confederacy, Tuesday Music, Sorosis, Lotus, Pioneer, and Woman's clubs. (Lakeland Public Library.)

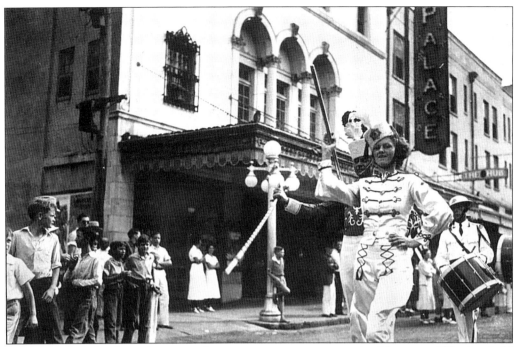

Downtown Lakeland was the scene of many community events and celebrations. Whether held in commemoration of the city's founding, the Fourth of July, Armistice Day, or other local festivals and events, the occasions almost always included parades that featured marching bands, festive floats, and participants of all ages. A lovely young woman in a sparkling white uniform served as the drum majorette for this parade in 1936, while a young boy dressed in a sailor suit rode his elaborately decorated bicycle. (Lakeland Public Library.)

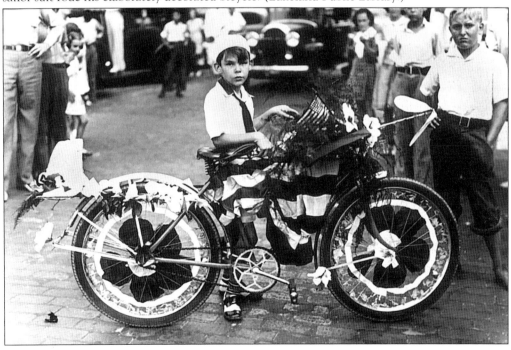

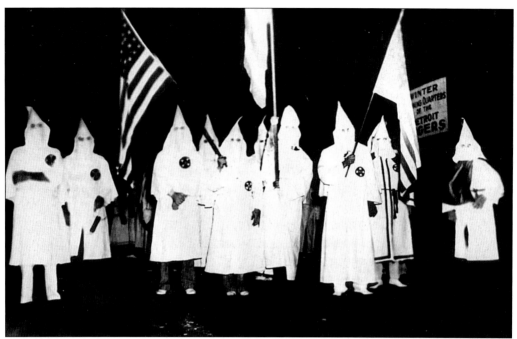

All parades were not happy, fun-filled occasions, however. On numerous occasions, African-Americans were confronted with the sight of the Ku Klux Klan marching in Lakeland's streets. The Klan had a long history in the state, dating from just after the Civil War when two Confederate veterans, William Stewart and Eldred J. Simpkins, organized the Florida Ku Klux Klan in the tiny town of Monticello. By the time that Daniel Starr Sanborn took these two photographs in 1938, the power of the Klan had waned to some degree in the United States. Florida was the exception, however, as the state continued to be a stronghold of the organization. (Lakeland Public Library.)

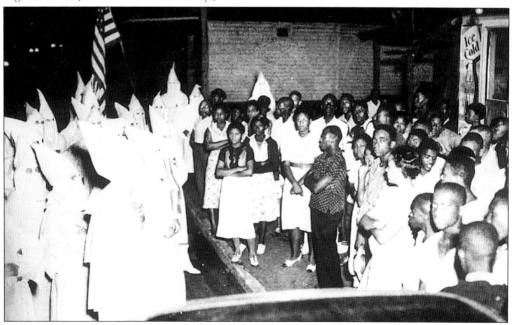

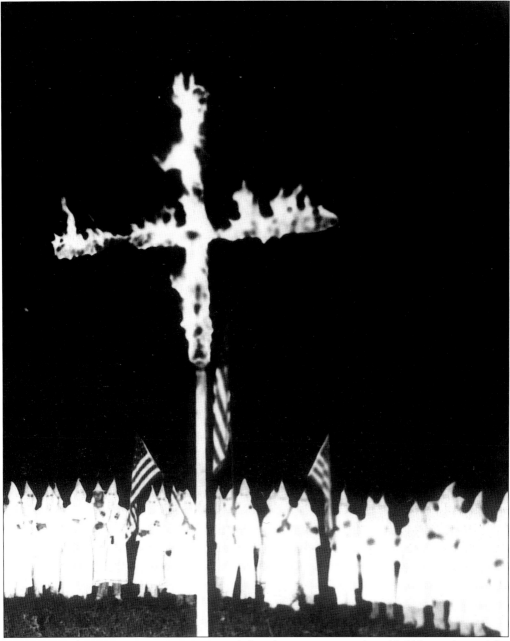

Even during the Depression, it was estimated that there were more than 30,000 members of the KKK in Florida. While the organization's largest units were located in Miami, Jacksonville, Orlando, and Tampa, the Central Florida citrus belt was especially dangerous for African-Americans. In the years between 1900 and 1930, the Klan lynched an average of almost five of every 10,000 African-Americans in Florida. Hooded night riders dressed in white sheets led a campaign marked by hatred, intimidation, and cross burnings—hallmarks of the organization. On August 30, 1938, a Ku Klux Klan parade along Dakota Avenue ended with a cross burning on the shores of Lake Mirror. Lakeland made the news for all of the wrong reasons when the photograph was featured in *Life* magazine. (Lakeland Public Library.)

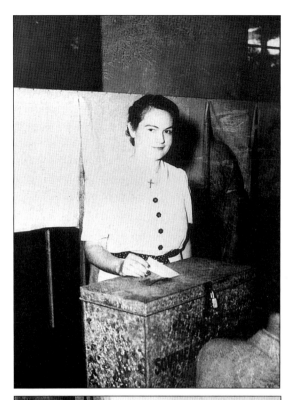

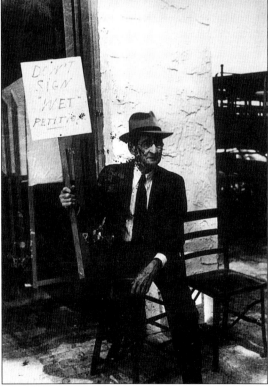

The U.S. Congress passed the Volstead Act in 1919, outlawing the sale and manufacture of intoxicating liquor nationwide. Bootleggers, rumrunners, speakeasies, and stills became common, however, as much of the nation tried to circumvent the law. In Lakeland, homemade moonshine from illicit stills hidden in local woods and swamps was also readily available. When Prohibition was repealed in 1933, certain areas of the country including Polk County elected to stay "dry," keeping the sale of alcohol illegal. Five years later, "wet" advocates attempted to place the issue on the ballot. As Lakeland's residents flocked to the polls, Miss Joyce Stoddard was the first to vote in precinct ten. With his sign in hand, G.K. Stratham advocated the idea of keeping Prohibition in place. (Lakeland Public Library.)

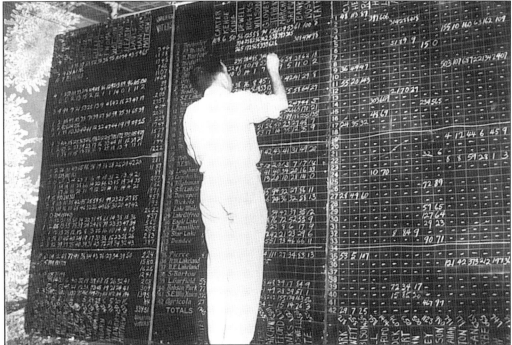

Dick Floyd of the *Lakeland Ledger* posted the results of the May 1938 election before announcing the outcome. The issue of allowing the sale of liquor within Polk County had once again been resoundingly defeated as voters chose to keep the county, and by default Lakeland, "dry." Not everyone was a believer, however. On July 31, 1938, newspapers featured a full page of photographs showing the destruction by police of illegal stills in the area. The issue would return to the ballot several times before Prohibition in Polk County would finally end 30 years after the repeal of the constitutional ban on alcohol. Voters approved the change by a narrow margin on May 21, 1963. (Lakeland Public Library.)

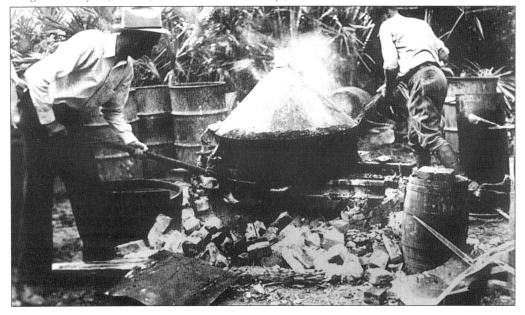

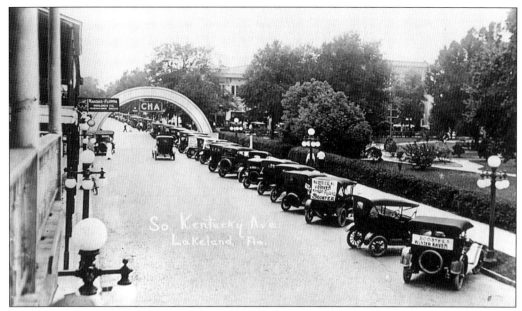

Cars belonging to the members of the Good Roads Association lined Main Street as the group mounted a frenzied campaign for improvement of highways in the area. Their efforts were successful. On June 1, 1916, voters approved a county bond issue of $1.5 million to pave with sheet asphalt some 217 miles of 9-foot-wide highway. Three years earlier, to awaken "good roads sentiments," the governor had called upon all residents to work on county roads for one day. (Lakeland Public Library.)

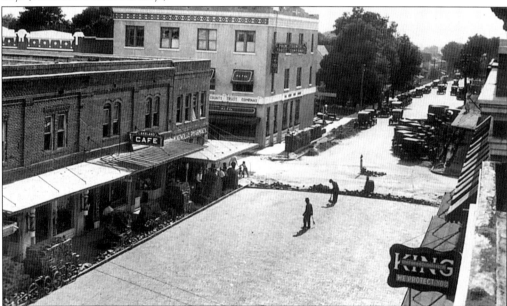

Traffic came to a halt in front of businesses along three blocks of East Main Street in 1924 as street crews re-bricked the road surface. Beginning in 1913, streets in the business district had been paved with bricks, while some residential streets were covered with asphalt. Bricks were a popular paving material in Florida, providing a durable road surface that did not crack in the summer heat, but still allowed water from rainstorms to drain. (Lakeland Public Library.)

In the late 1930s, other street improvements took place in Lakeland. In an effort designed to fill the dual purposes of returning men to work while at the same time bettering local communities, the federal government funded a number of Works Progress Administration projects. One such endeavor included the construction of a veritable forest of street markers, (below). Made of cast concrete, the markers were painted with the names of Lakeland's streets and then installed throughout the town. One hundred and four workers were hired at a cost of $37,942 for eight months to work on various city enhancements. The WPA also funded a sewing project that employed African-American women. (Lakeland Public Library.)

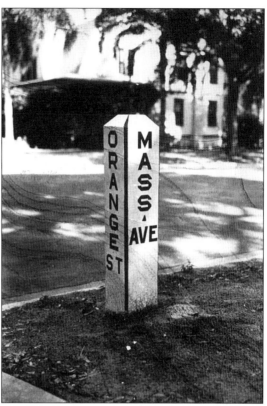

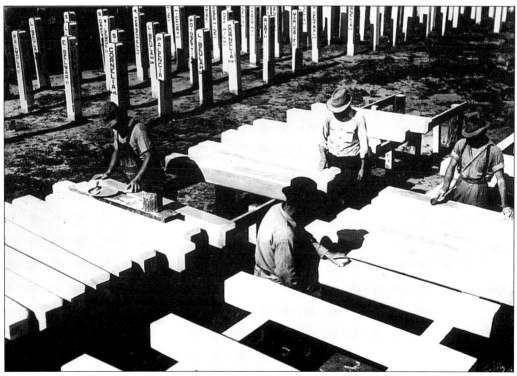

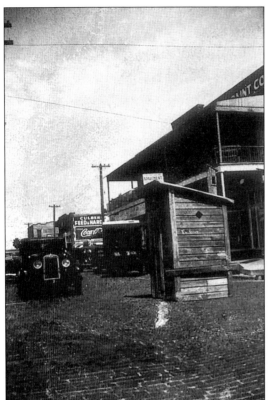

An unexpected sight on Pine Street in 1938, this wooden privy was the Depression-era equivalent of today's portable toilets. Although less than scenic in appearance, the privy had been provided for the convenience of the Works Progress Administration laborers who were employed on various construction projects in Lakeland. (Lakeland Public Library.)

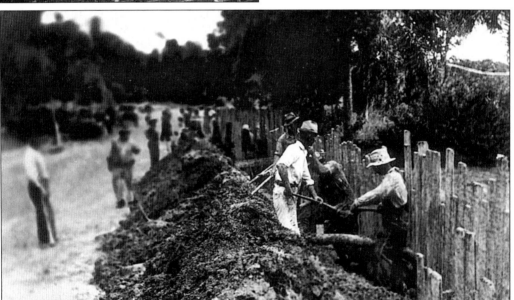

In addition to construction work on a number of buildings in town, the Works Progress Administration also hired men to lay the lines for the Lake Hollingsworth sewer system. Using picks and shovels, WPA workers had already laid approximately 2,000 feet of sewer pipe by September 1938. Although the backbreaking labor was hot and dirty, the wages earned represented the only income for many households during hard times. (Lakeland Public Library.)

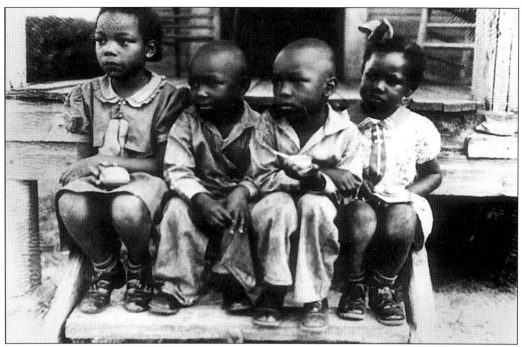

The Great Depression did not discriminate—people of all races, backgrounds, and socioeconomic levels were affected. As was true across the nation, many of Lakeland's residents were unemployed. Local banks failed and stores closed. School employees took a ten-percent pay cut in April 1932, but at least they still had jobs. Perhaps hardest hit were the children who really did not understand the economic realities of the situation, but who suffered nonetheless. For them, new clothes and toys became increasingly infrequent as their families labored to supply the basic necessities of life. For some children, including the young boys in the lower photograph, new glasses to correct vision problems were supplied as a result of the local Lions Club Sight Conservation project. (Lakeland Public Library.)

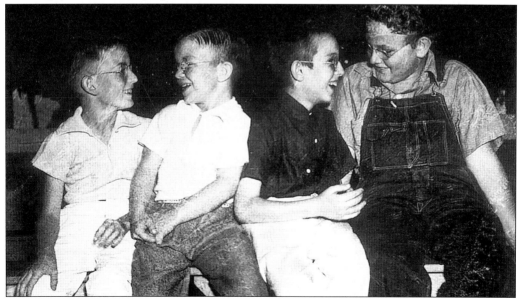

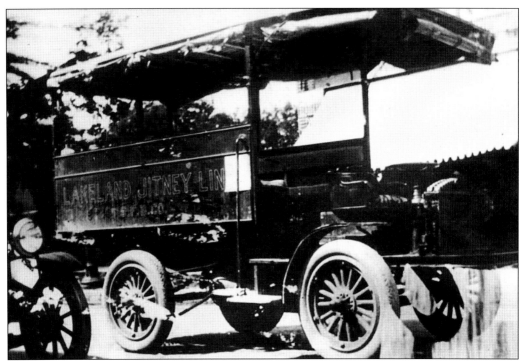

Mass transit in Lakeland has taken various forms over the years. For just a nickel, passengers could climb aboard a Lakeland Jitney Lines vehicle and ride through the Dixieland neighborhood, along Kentucky Avenue and Main Street to South Florida Avenue, over to Lake Hollingsworth, and back around Lake Morton to Main Street. In that one respect at least, those were truly the "good old days." (Lakeland Public Library.)

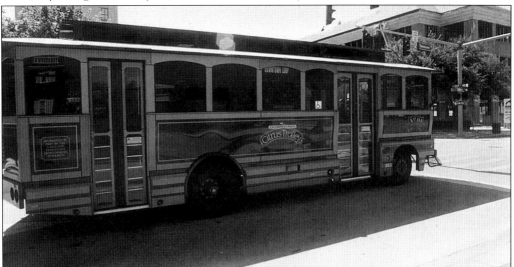

Anyone who says bargains no longer exist is just plain wrong—at least with regard to a ride on the Downtown Citrus Trolley. Making a "lunchtime loop" through Lakeland's business district every day between 11 a.m. and 2 p.m., the gold and green trolley provides a quick and easy way to get around the downtown, grab a bite to eat, or do some lunch-hour shopping. And best of all, the trolley ride does not even cost a nickel—it's free! (Authors' Collection.)

Four
FIGHTING THE GOOD FIGHT

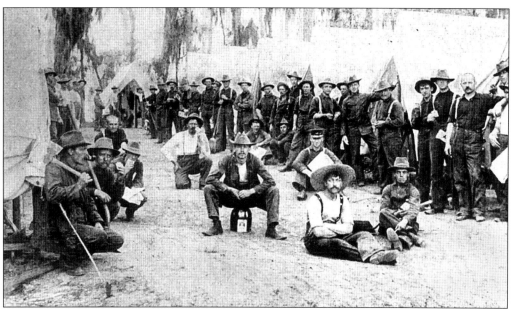

Tiny Lakeland played an important role during the Spanish-American War. From 6,000 to 9,000 troops are estimated to have called Lakeland their temporary home between May and August 1898. Units based there included the 10th U.S. Cavalry, 2nd Massachusetts Infantry, 1st U.S. Cavalry, 71st New York Volunteers, 1st Ohio Volunteer Cavalry, 3rd U.S. Cavalry, and the 9th Cavalry. Nearby Tampa was already overcrowded with soldiers awaiting transportation to Cuba. When the troops were finally called for departure, an existing rail network would allow easy movement from Lakeland to Tampa. Lakeland also offered the additional advantages of open land, numerous lakes to provide a ready supply of water, and a higher elevation that was believed to be healthier. (Lakeland Public Library.)

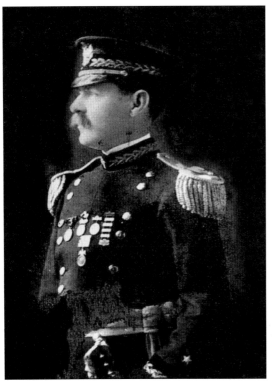

In an entry in his diary, Major Frederick E. Pierce of Company L, 2nd Regiment Massachusetts Infantry, described his arrival in Lakeland on May 16, 1898. Of their camp, Pierce wrote, "This spot is charming and the site selected an ideal one, situated on the picturesque banks of Lake Morton in a grove of tall white oaks whose drooping branches are festooned with great bunches of beautiful Spanish moss." (Lakeland Public Library.)

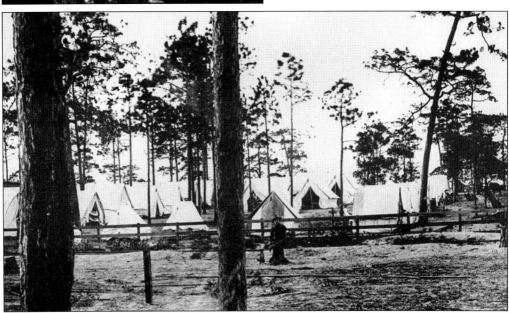

This image of a 10th Cavalry campsite offered a picture of serenity that did not match reality. The African-American soldiers of the 10th frequently encountered something for which they were unprepared—Jim Crow laws. Problems often arose; at least one black soldier shot and killed a Lakeland civilian during a confrontation. In some of the worst fighting in Cuba, however, men of the all-black unit were said to be "among the deadliest fighters of the war." Five men of the 10th Cavalry were awarded the Medal of Honor. (Lakeland Public Library.)

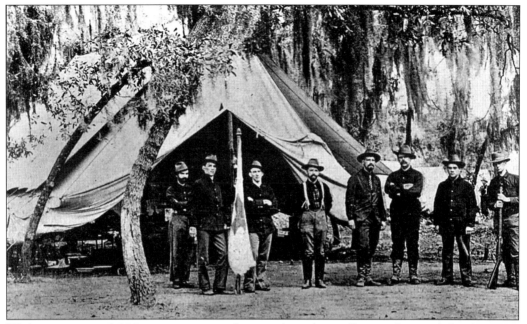

With as many as 9,000 troops encamped in a relatively small area, the need for the camp hospital was paramount. Men died of pneumonia, while others suffered from accidents, illnesses, and other non-life threatening maladies. Bites from snakes and insects were common. The men complained of heat, rain, rattlesnakes, flies, and mosquitoes. The hospital could not help with most of the problems—they were simply part of daily outdoor life in the Florida summer. (Lakeland Public Library.)

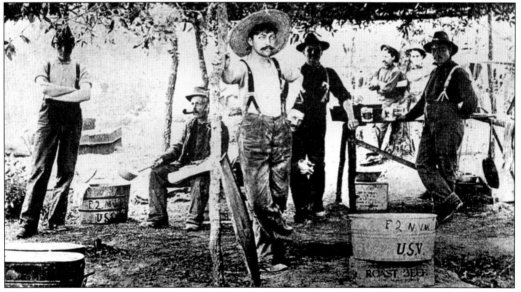

It's been said, "An army travels on its stomach." Troops had to be fed. While rudimentary at best, this camp kitchen did just that. The local population also helped in the care and feeding of the soldiers. In his diary, one trooper recalled Sunday mornings when they "would go out to an old colored lady's shack where she would bake us some of the finest hot cakes I ever tasted, with 'lasses and coffee. The price was 20 cents." (Lakeland Public Library.)

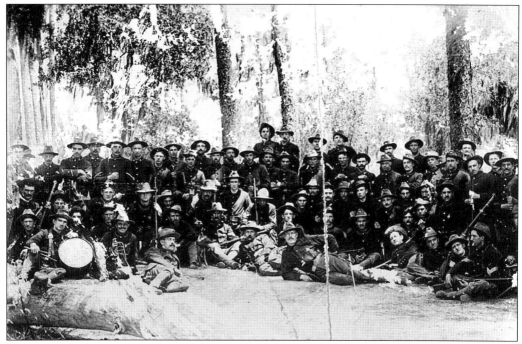

A group from the 71st Regiment of the New York Volunteers posed for this photograph in May 1898. The troops, commanded by Capt. Malcolm Rafferty, arrived in Lakeland on May 17, establishing a campsite on the shore of Lake Morton. They did not have long to enjoy Lakeland—on May 31 they headed for Tampa and then Cuba. (Lakeland Public Library.)

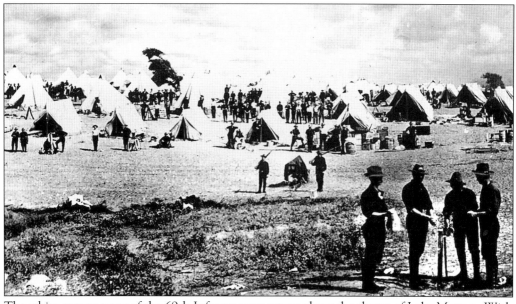

The white canvas tents of the 69th Infantry were set up along the shores of Lake Morton. With typical military efficiency, despite the intense summer heat, troops garbed in wool pants and flannel shirts spent most of the day drilling in preparation for war in Cuba. The cool water of Lake Morton must have offered the men a welcome respite after hours spent training in the Florida sun. (Lakeland Public Library.)

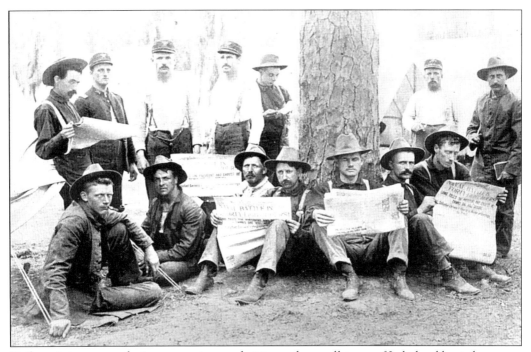

Daily training, camp duties, recreation, and visits to the small town of Lakeland kept the troops busy. One of the most important aspects of camp life, however, was reading newspaper accounts of war in the far-off Philippines. Of even greater significance was the action in Cuba, something that these men expected to experience firsthand. (Lakeland Public Library.)

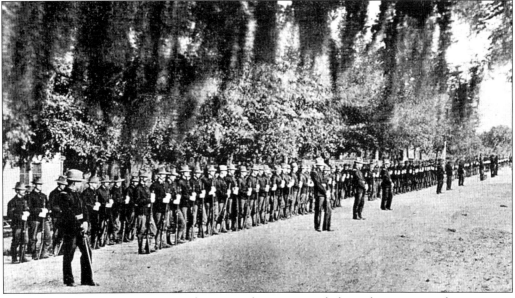

Men of the 2nd Regiment Massachusetts Infantry trooped the colors as part of an evening parade during their brief stay in Lakeland. Arriving on May 16, they made a camp on Lake Morton their temporary home. On May 20, they were ordered to Tampa. By the end of August 1898, Lakeland was but a memory for the men of the various units who had briefly called the town home. Battle called, and they were off to war. (Lakeland Public Library.)

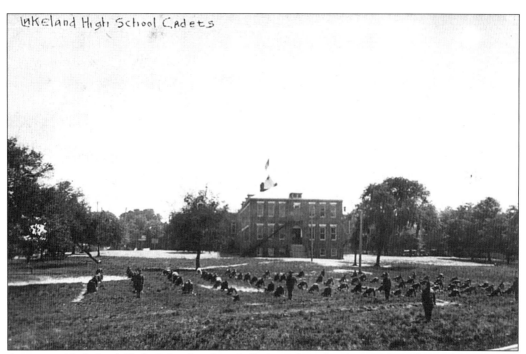

A group of Lakeland High School cadets drilled on the school grounds and marched through the town's streets. As America prepared to enter the European conflict that would escalate into World War I, speeches in Munn Park by dignitaries such as Teddy Roosevelt helped to fan the flames of enthusiasm for the war. Like others across the nation, Lakeland's young men were filled with patriotic fervor. Another military group, the Lakeland Home Guards, had formed in 1914. Within a few years, its rolls had increased from 20 to nearly 100 members. Lakeland sent many of her young men off to war. Hugh Sims, L.W. Yarnall Jr., Woodson Williams, Bert Lane, and William E. Ferreand were among those who lost their lives. Others, including Leonard Riggins, returned as heroes. (Lakeland Public Library.)

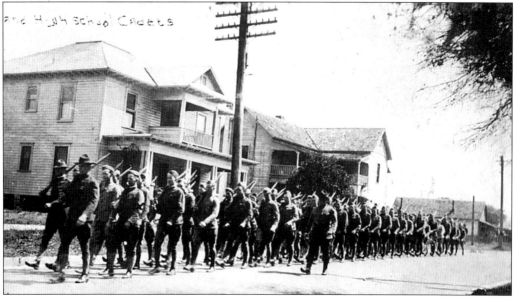

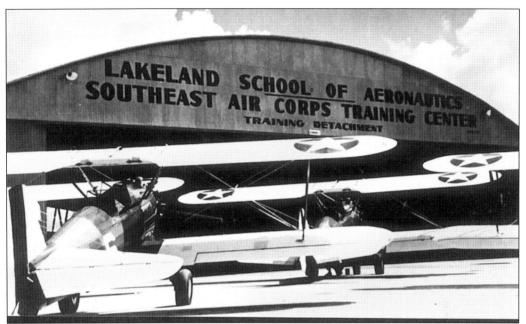

A flight of bi-winged PT-17 trainers lined up in front of the hangar at the Lakeland School of Aeronautics, to be renamed as the Lodwick School of Aeronautics in July 1942. The objective of the civilian school was to provide flight training during World War II to cadets of both the American Army Air Forces and the British Royal Air Force. By the end of the war, approximately 6,000 trainees had graduated from Lodwick. (Lakeland Public Library.)

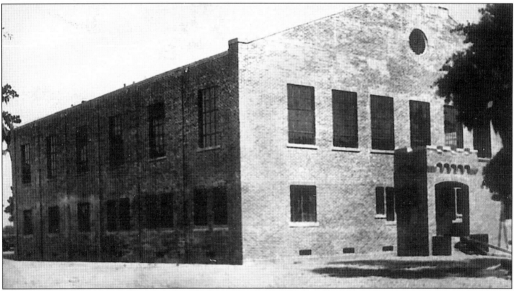

When the first classes of aviation cadets reported for training at Lodwick, many of the facilities were not yet completed. For that reason, ground school was conducted downtown in the Lakeland Armory. The ground school segment of training included 85 to 140 hours in navigation, aircraft engines, aircraft identification, code, weather, mathematics, and chemical warfare defense. Each day the cadets spent three to four hours in classrooms before heading to the field for flight training. (Lakeland Public Library.)

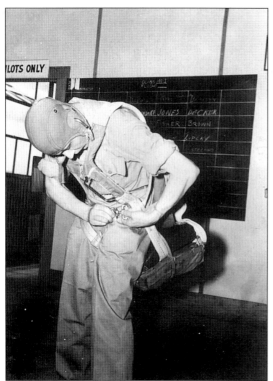

On September 18, 1940, the first class of 40 flight cadets reported to Lakeland for primary flight training. Soon the average class size had grown to 180 cadets. The 10-week primary training program consisted of a minimum of 60 hours of flight time. The flying was both dual and solo, and included at least five hours on the ground in a Link trainer. Not all of the cadets made it through the training; approximately 30 percent were eliminated from the program. (Lakeland Public Library.)

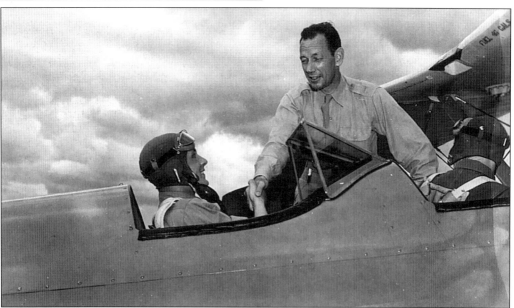

Royal Air Force flight cadets began training at Lodwick on June 9, 1941, with a class of 90 British airmen. Because of Britain's tremendous need for pilots, the school stopped training Americans to devote all of its efforts to the RAF. Sitting in the cockpit of his trainer, John Staples received a congratulatory handshake from Captain Harry Copeland, director of the school. The young man from London, England, had been the first RAF flight cadet to solo. (Lakeland Public Library.)

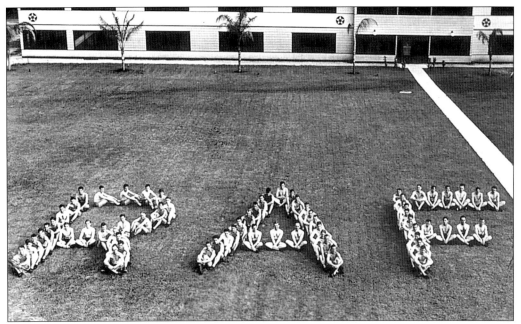
Dressed in exercise attire, a group of Royal Air Force flight cadets formed the letters "RAF" in front of their barracks at Lodwick. Slight changes had to be made to the training program to accommodate the British students, but for the most part there were no problems. In fact, the people of Lakeland warmly embraced the British cadets, making the homesick young men feel as welcome as possible. (Lakeland Public Library.)

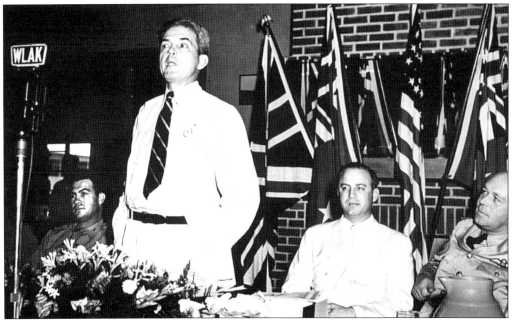
The first group of Royal Air Force cadets graduated from the Lodwick School of Aeronautics at Lakeland on August 16, 1941. Spessard L. Holland, Florida's governor, was on hand to address the RAF cadets and to present each man with his hard-earned diploma. Seated on the platform next to Governor Holland was Albert Lodwick, owner of the school. (Lakeland Public Library.)

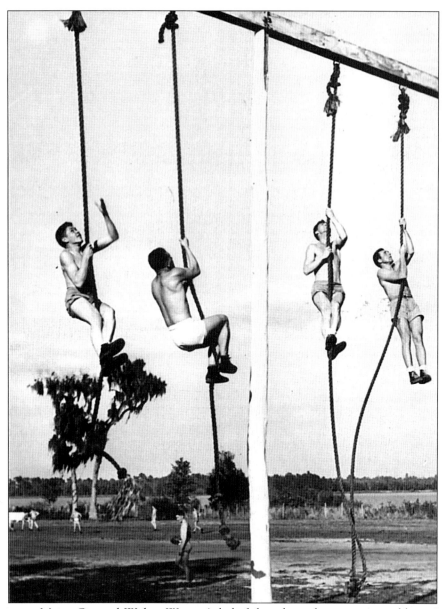

Since it was Major General Walter Weaver's belief that the military was not able to "entrust expensive planes to men who may fail physically," training at the Lodwick School of Aeronautics meant more than flying airplanes. With days that began early and usually lasted late into the nights, physical training was a very large and important part of the instruction program. Cadets ran obstacle courses and spent hours each day on exercises that would improve their upper body strength. There were also exercises designed to improve peripheral vision to make pilots more effective at spotting enemy aircraft. Since Lodwick was a civilian school with few military personnel on the base, it fell to civilian contractors to provide the physical training equipment designed by the military to hone a flight cadet's physical and mental fitness. Recreational physical fitness activities were also encouraged with facilities available for all sports including swimming, football, baseball, and track. Obviously Lakeland's weather was perfect for year-round sporting events. (Lakeland Public Library.)

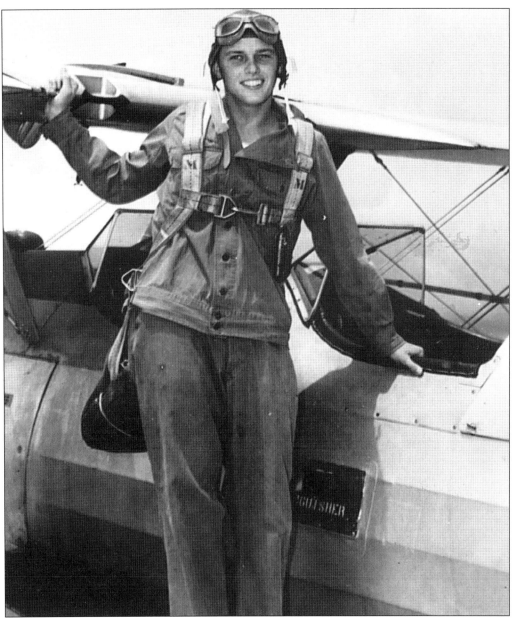

After the United States entered World War II in December 1941, the training of American flight cadets resumed at the Lodwick School of Aeronautics. From June until October 1942, American and British flight cadets trained together. The men got along famously, as the community of Lakeland welcomed them all. As the cadets became part of the city's life, it was a rare weekend they were not invited to dine with local families. After the last class of RAF cadets graduated in October 1942, the school devoted the training program exclusively to Americans. During the war, Lodwick's civilian school fell under the control of the Army Air Forces, 60th Flying Training Detachment. Paid $18.70 per flying hour by the Army Air Forces, the school was highly profitable. According to audited financial statements for 1942, the combined income for the partnership of Albert Lodwick and his wife Dorothy was in excess of $300,000. (Lakeland Public Library.)

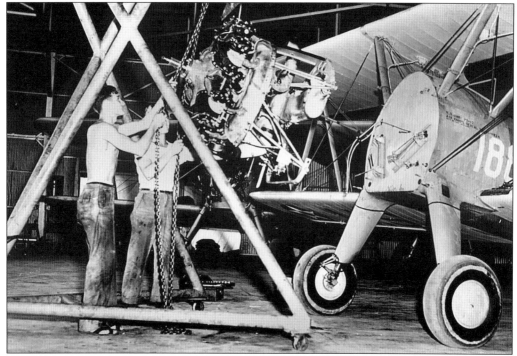

The pilots received all of the glory, but the airplanes did not fly without engines. Mechanics were obviously of great importance. Men and women, many of whom were recruited locally, worked long hours to ensure that the airplanes were safe and ready to fly. Each day there were hundreds of tasks to be performed. Airplanes needed to be refueled, repaired, and checked out before the day's training began. (Lakeland Public Library.)

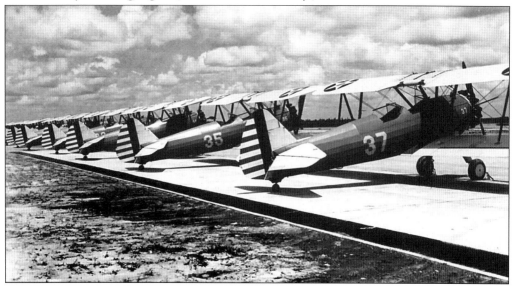

Stearman PT-17 Kaydets were lined up and ready to be flown at the Lodwick School of Aeronautics. When the school first opened in 1940, there were only 25 of the two-seat airplanes at the facility. By the time the school in Lakeland closed in August 1945, the fleet of Stearman PT-17s numbered in the hundreds. (Lakeland Public Library.)

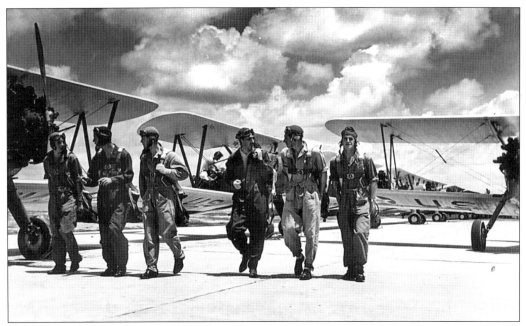
At the end of the ten-week primary training program, final flight tests were given, after which cadets were transferred to another civilian school or military base. By the time the Lodwick School of Aeronautics closed, thousands of flight cadets, both British and American, had been trained at the school. At the same time, an equivalent number had been through the training program at a second Lodwick facility in nearby Avon Park. (Lakeland Public Library.)

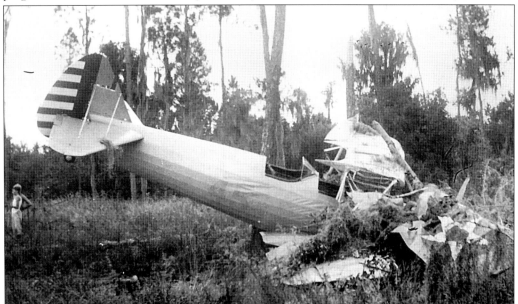
The United States Army Air Forces promised the best flight training in the world, regardless of whether it was provided by the military or by civilian contractors. Instructors taught emergency landing procedures and worked tirelessly to ensure that flying was safe. Unfortunately, pilot training was dangerous work. No matter how hard instructors worked, airplanes did crash. Five flight cadets died in training at the Lodwick School of Aeronautics. (Lakeland Public Library.)

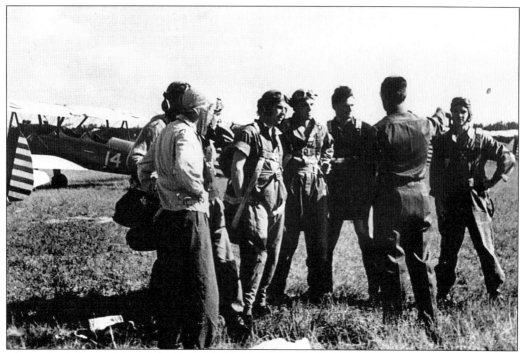

The contribution of the Lodwick School of Aeronautics to Lakeland's economy was not only significant, but also much needed after the Depression. The school employed hundreds of local residents and most of the money generated by the facility flowed into Lakeland. After the last class graduated on August 1, 1945, contract #W33-038, AC-3470 between the War Department and the Lodwick School had been cancelled, terminating operations as of August 1945. As military personnel transferred out, local employees sought new jobs. Although it was just a formality, the Lodwick School of Aeronautics officially ceased to exist with the issuance of a final certificate of corporate dissolution on April 7, 1949. (Lakeland Public Library.)

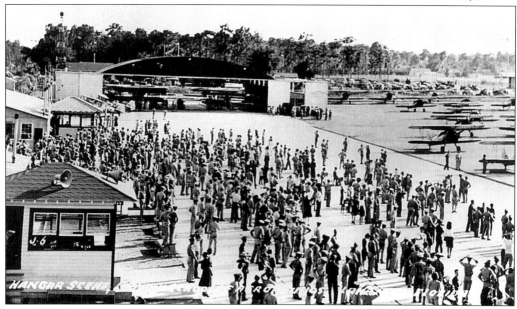

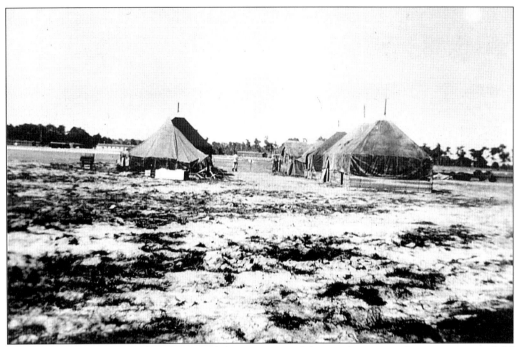

On April 21, 1941, Works Progress Administration laborers began work on a new airfield southwest of Lakeland. Although it was planned as the city's second municipal airport, the military eventually took over Drane Field, renaming the facility as Lakeland Army Air Field. On May 9, 1942, the Army Air Forces announced the base's opening; eight days later, troops began to arrive at a base that was not yet ready. (Lakeland Public Library.)

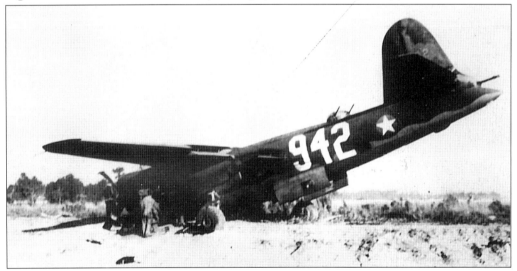

Created from a cow pasture and woods, the new airfield served as a sub-base of Tampa's MacDill Army Air Field. Lakeland Army Air Field's purpose during World War II was to provide "third-phase training activities of combat crews." Over the life of the airfield, practically every type of military aircraft, including heavy bombers and fighter aircraft, was seen flying in the vicinity of Lakeland each day. With that number of aircraft, accidents were bound to happen—and they did. (Lakeland Public Library.)

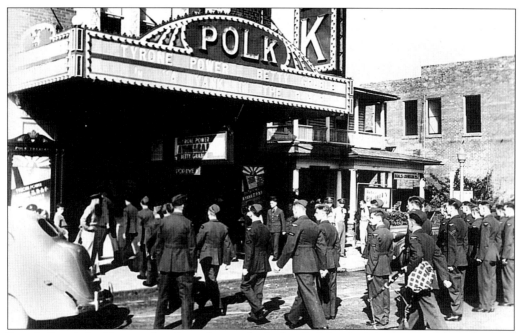

British Royal Air Force cadets from the nearby Lodwick School of Aeronautics flocked to the Polk Theatre on a Sunday afternoon. First-run movies, serials, and newsreels chronicling the progress of the war in Europe and the Pacific were in demand. Lakeland's Polk, Lake, and Palace theatres were used as sites for bond and victory loan drives as well. (Lakeland Public Library.)

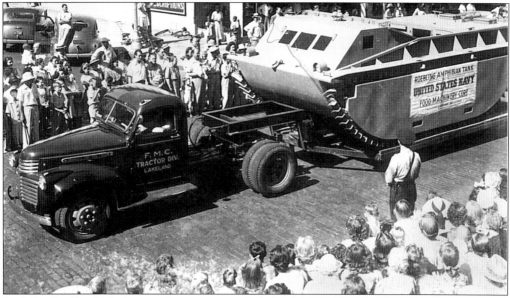

Built by the Food Machinery Corporation in Lakeland, a Roebling landing vehicle named the Water Buffalo rolled through downtown streets in 1942. The vehicle's lineage could be traced to the Alligator, designed and built by Clearwater's Donald Roebling to rescue flood victims. When the Food Machinery Corporation realized that their peacetime manufacturing would be halted, the company retooled to build military vehicles. Nationwide, the company produced approximately 10,000 landing vehicles of different designs. (Lakeland Public Library.)

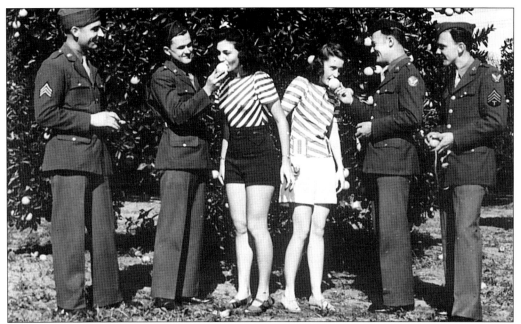

Whether flight cadets at the Lodwick School of Aeronautics or Army Air Forces personnel at Lakeland Army Air Field, all of the young men received royal treatment from local residents. Every Lakeland mother who had a son or daughter in the military wanted to provide the same hospitality she hoped her child was receiving wherever he or she was stationed. Of course, attention from attractive, young women was always welcome. (Lakeland Public Library.)

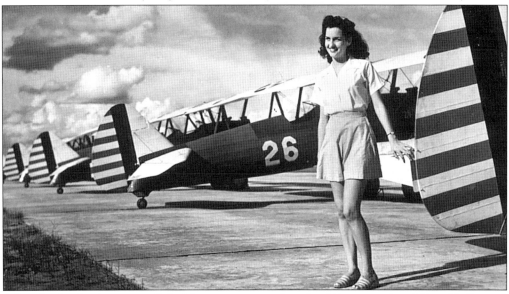

Albert Lodwick, always mindful of the importance of good publicity, employed Stan Hedberg as his public relations officer. Several local photographers including Dan Sanborn and Duane Perkins were constantly on call to record scenes of daily military life, significant events, or the visits of important dignitaries. Few visits to the Lodwick School of Aeronautics were ever better received than that of Ivie Anne Hall, the winner of a local beauty contest in 1942. (Lakeland Public Library.)

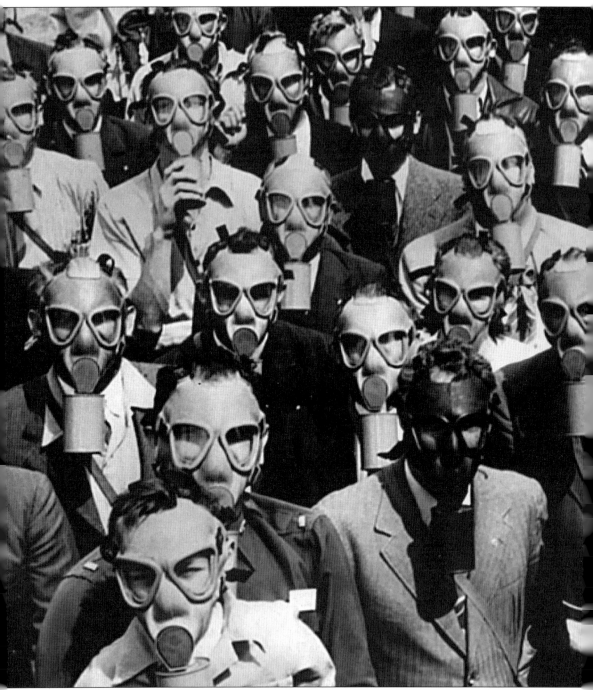

During World War II, the citizens of Lakeland did just as other Americans—they prepared for war. In this photograph taken by Dan Sanborn, a group of local residents, young and old, donned gas masks in preparation for what they feared most—an attack by Germany. Once occupied by tourists, rooms at the Terrace and New Florida now housed soldiers and airmen as military personnel filled Lakeland's hotels. As one government official put it, "The best hotel room is none too good for the American soldier." With a war being waged, Lakeland residents

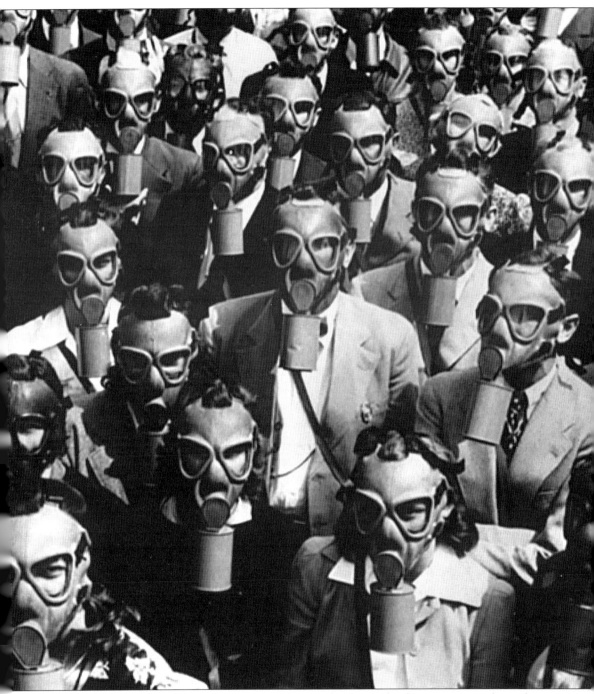

of all ages wanted to help. Scrap drives netted thousands of pounds of paper, rags, and metal to be recycled. Civil defense workers performed various duties, relieving others for military service. From the rooftops of tall buildings, volunteers scanned the skies for enemy aircraft. Rationing became a way of life. Every man, woman, and child in Lakeland had a ration book containing stamps that determined what they could buy. (Lakeland Public Library.)

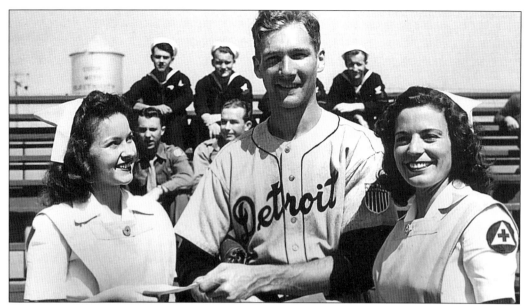

Hal Newhauser, the Detroit Tigers' ace left-handed pitcher, posed for a publicity photo with two civil defense workers at a spring training game in Lakeland during the war. Baseball players who had not enlisted in the military provided much needed entertainment for those on the home front and frequently participated in bond drives. President Roosevelt had earlier voiced his sentiments on the subject, saying, "I honestly think that it would be best for the country to keep baseball going." (Lakeland Public Library.)

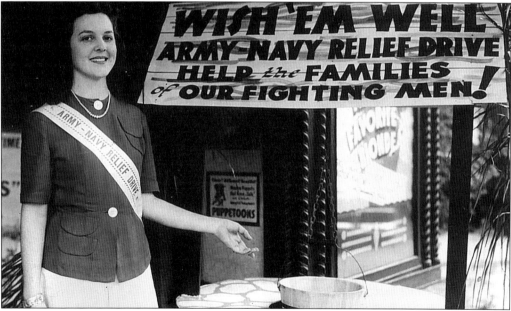

A volunteer collected money for the Army-Navy Relief Drive at a Lakeland theatre. Organized to provide financial assistance to military widows and orphans, the group also made certain that the men and women serving overseas were not forgotten by sending small gifts such as playing cards and toiletries. Nationwide, the proceeds generated by sporting events, wishing wells, and other activities raised thousands of dollars for the fund. (Lakeland Public Library.)

Five
HARD AT WORK

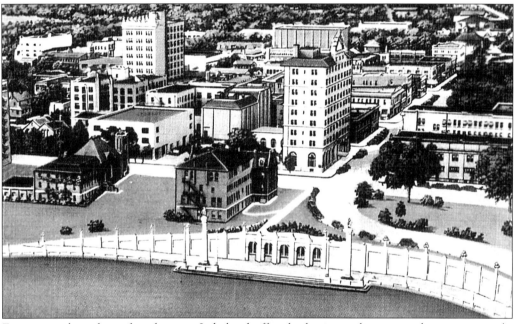

From its earliest days of settlement, Lakeland offered a business climate conducive to growth. Enhanced by an excellent rail system that made the transportation of people and products an easy and convenient matter, the city offered many of the amenities needed to attract businesses. There were electric lights, water works, fire protection, a telephone system, an ice plant, and several banks. Year-round good weather coupled with an abundance of available land made truck farming, citrus growing, and cattle ranching lucrative endeavors. The quite profitable business of phosphate mining flourished in the area. Just a few years after the arrival of the first settlers, Lakeland's Main Street was lined with thriving businesses. During the boom era of the 1920s, the downtown saw rapid growth with the construction of the Terrace and New Florida hotels, the Oates Building, and the 10-story Marble Arcade. While the city's skyline has changed over the years, Lakeland is still the business and financial center of Polk County. (Lakeland Public Library.)

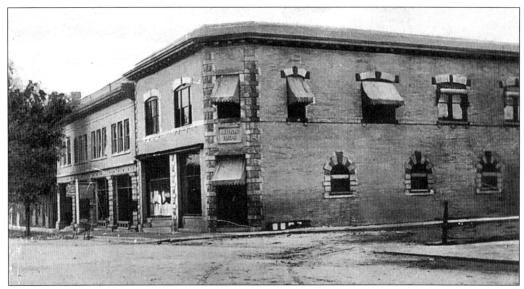

As were many of the buildings in early Lakeland, construction of the Munn and Drane Buildings, located on the corner of Main Street and Kentucky Avenue, was financed by the Lakeland Building and Improvement Company. Owned by Morris J. Munn, Herbert J. Drane, and several other partners, the company hired W.B. Talley to design the structures. Constructed in 1903 as part of a brick business block, the Munn and Drane Buildings were expanded in 1907 with the construction of the Munn Annex. (Lakeland Public Library.)

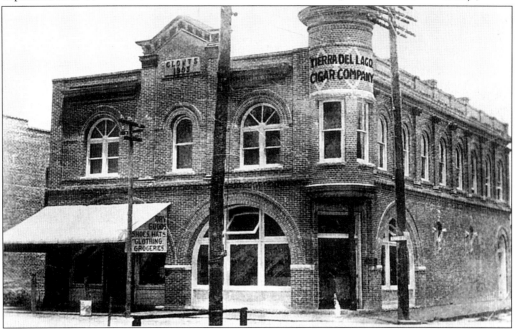

Without a doubt, the most distinctive feature of the brick Clonts Building is its three-story turret. Samuel L.A. Clonts, a four-term mayor of Lakeland, constructed the impressive structure on the corner of East Pine Street and North Kentucky Avenue in 1903. The Clonts Building has been used for a number of purposes, including a retail shop and as the sales office for one of several cigar manufacturers that operated in Lakeland. (Lakeland Public Library.)

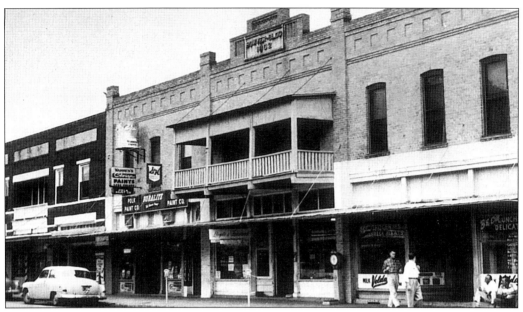

By the time this photograph was taken in the 1950s, this brick business block had already had a long life. Erected in 1902 by Napoleon B. Bowyer, the Bowyer Building at North Kentucky Avenue and Pine Street was originally a freestanding structure that housed a retail establishment on the first floor and a hotel on the second. It was not long, however, before buildings were constructed on both sides. Still in use today, the Bowyer Building is the oldest remaining commercial brick building in Lakeland. (Lakeland Public Library.)

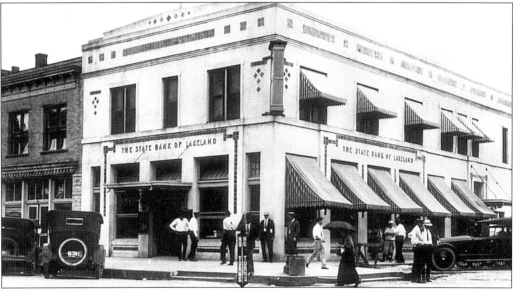

The State Bank of Lakeland served local as well as seasonal residents in 1925. Originally chartered as the State Bank of Fort Meade, the institution relocated to Lakeland in 1902. E.O. Flood, the bank's cashier, and John F. Cox, the assistant cashier, both had political aspirations. While a resident of Fort Meade, Flood had been the city clerk, treasurer, and assessor. In Lakeland, he served several terms as a city councilman. John Cox was elected as mayor of Lakeland seven times. (Lakeland Public Library.)

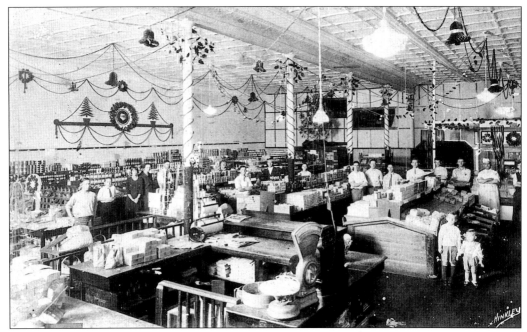

The Grocerteria, located on the corner of Kentucky Avenue and Pine Street, was billed as the first self-service grocery store in Florida. Originally owned by Daniel C. Boswell and J.E. Miller, the general store offered Lakeland's shoppers everything from soup to nuts. Hinkley's Studio, boasting of "the only panoramic camera in Polk County," took this photograph of the gaily-decorated interior of the Grocerteria in 1925. (Lakeland Public Library.)

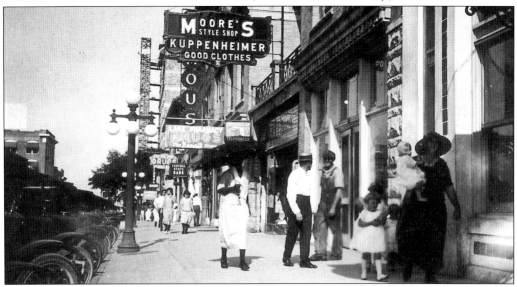

Earl Morgan Savage photographed Moore's Style Shop at 207 East Main Street in the mid-1920s. The haberdashery sold all types of clothing including robes, ties, hats, shirts, and pants. Hyperbole in advertising is nothing new, as an advertisement for Moore's proved. "Our caps overtop the world in style and satisfaction. Our varieties of colors and patterns overtop competitors." Not surprisingly, the store advertised itself as "Lakeland's Best Clothes Shop." (Lakeland Public Library.)

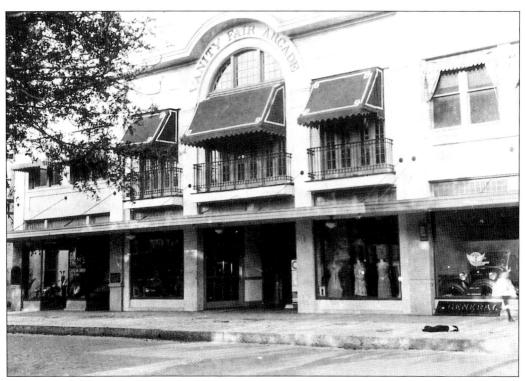

Constructed during the 1920s, the Vanity Fair Arcade was yet one more example of boom-era architecture in Lakeland. Located on Tennessee Avenue, the structure featured an open arcade that ran through the building from one block to the next. Located inside the Vanity Fair Arcade were several businesses, including George Emmon's Shoe Store, the Vogue Hat Shop, Bates Women's Clothing, and a coffee shop. (Lakeland Public Library.)

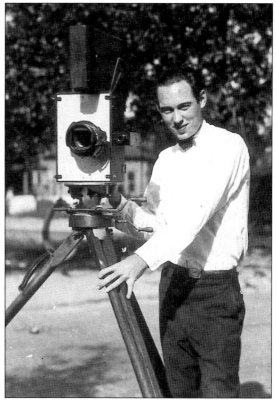

Little is known about the activities of Earl Morgan Savage other than during the few short years that he called Lakeland home. Savage had a shop in the Vanity Fair Arcade and a residence on Kentucky Avenue. While operating Savage's Camera Shop during 1924 and 1925, he actively documented Lakeland's streets and buildings, amassing a large photographic collection that is still invaluable to researchers today. (Lakeland Public Library.)

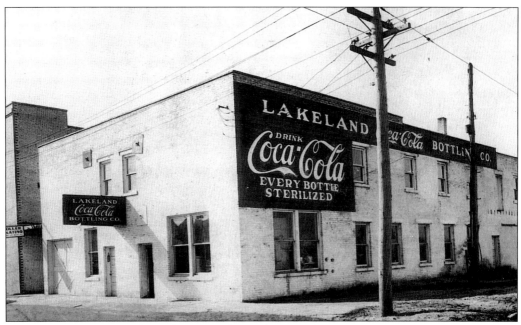

By the late 1920s, the Lakeland Coca-Cola Bottling Company was just one of more than 5,000 soft drink bottlers in the United States who were responsible for turning out a consistent product for the Atlanta, Georgia, Coca-Cola Company. Locally owned by W.L. Smith and managed by Ernest G. Kemp, the bottling works advertised on the side of the building that "Every bottle is sterilized." Each day employees would collect ingredients that included citrate caffeine, vanilla, extract of cola, sugar, caramel, water, and a secret mixture of fruit oils and spices known as "7-X." These would be mixed together in large vats to produce a sweet and sticky syrup. When combined with seltzer water, the result would be a drink that would be described as "The Pause That Refreshes." (Lakeland Public Library.)

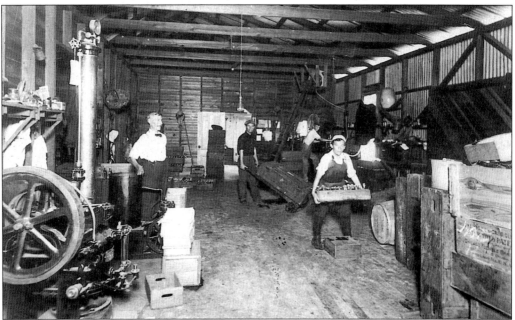

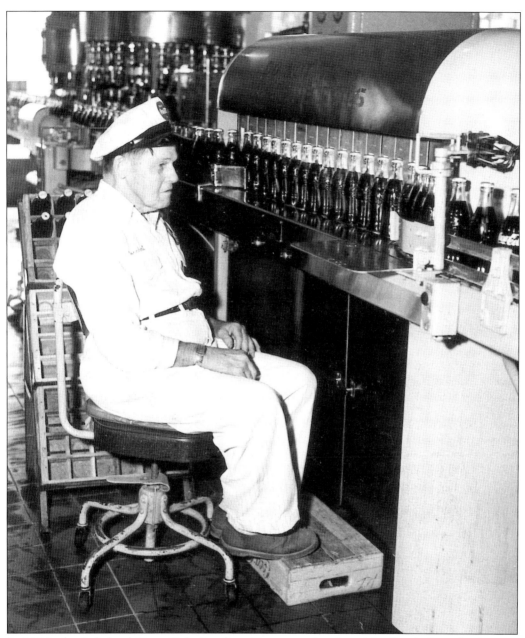

In 1936, the Lakeland Coca-Cola Bottling Company abandoned its South Lincoln Avenue facility for a more modern structure. Overlooking Lake Mirror, the new two-story, red brick bottling plant on East Main Street cost $30,000 to build. By the 1960s when this photograph was taken, the bottling process had been completely mechanized—a far cry from the days when the soft drink was brewed in tubs, featured cocaine as an ingredient, and was touted as a medicinal drink. Featuring a formula nearly 100 years old, the Coca-Cola Company was telling customers that their soft drink was "The real thing" and that "Things go better with Coke." After the bottling works closed in 1972, the building was used for several purposes. Thanks to the efforts of Historic Lakeland, Inc., the building today serves as the administrative headquarters of the Lakeland Fire Department. (Lakeland Public Library.)

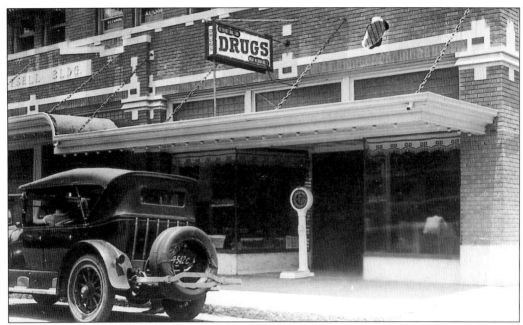

One thing that the citizens of Lakeland did not lack was an abundance of drugstores. As early as 1905, residents could choose between Lake Pharmacy and Boswell & Company Druggists. Owned by Dr. W.R. Groover, Lake Pharmacy was located in the Kentucky Building. Rows of wooden shelves and glass-enclosed cases held patent medicines, toilet articles, stationery, cigars, pipes, bric-a-brac, and many novelty items. M.F. Huntly, O.D., had an office at the Boswell store where he claimed to practice the "most advanced methods in the examination of the eye and in the correction of defects such as presbyopia, myopia, hypermetropia, strabismus, and muscular asthemopia." As the population increased, so did the number of drugstores. By the late 1920s, downtown Lakeland could claim the Magnolia Pharmacy, Jewetts, Walgreen Drugs, Lake Pharmacy, City Drug Store, and more. (Lakeland Public Library.)

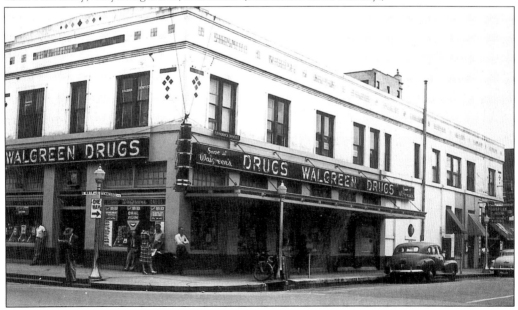

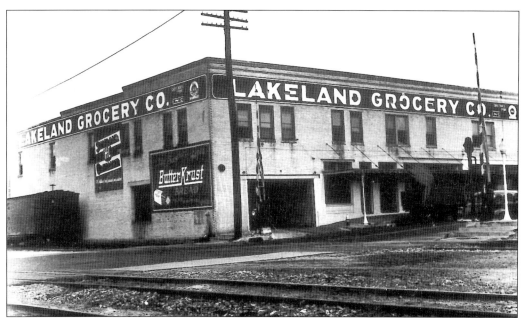

Owned by A.J. Powell, the Lakeland Grocery Company was one of a small chain of grocery stores called "All American Stores." Unfortunately for Mr. Powell, a marketing revolution lurked just around the corner. George W. Jenkins opened his first Publix grocery store in Winter Park in 1930; ten years later, he opened the first "food palace." Housed in distinctive Art Deco buildings constructed of glass, marble, and stucco, Jenkins's stores featured eight-foot-wide aisles, frozen food cases, music, florescent lights, and air conditioning. No longer considered a chore, grocery shopping at Publix was now an outing. The company opened a 125,000-square-foot warehouse in Lakeland in 1951. Today Publix is one of the largest supermarket chains in America; Lakeland is home to several Publix distribution and manufacturing centers. (Lakeland Public Library.)

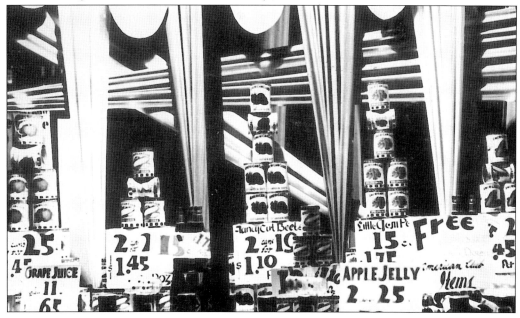

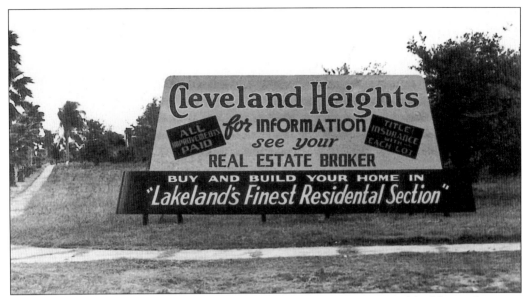

A billboard near Lake Hollingsworth exhorted homebuyers to "Buy and build your home in 'Lakeland's Finest Residential Section.'" H.A. Stahl Properties, a Cleveland, Ohio, real estate development company, purchased 560 acres on the side south of Lake Hollingsworth to launch its very upscale Cleveland Heights community in 1924. Work continued for the next two years on the development that was intended to have 1,200 residences and a golf course. (Lakeland Public Library.)

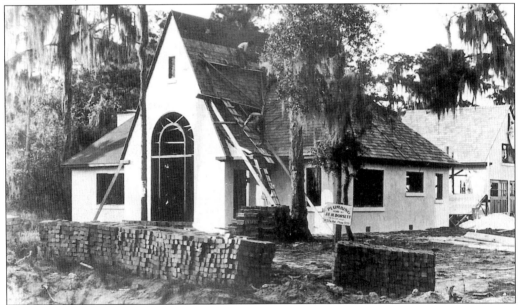

In 1925, the Highland Club and its 18-hole, 150-acre golf course opened. Lots that included an interest in the golf course and clubhouse sold for as much as $2,000, with the homes among Lakeland's most costly. Nearly 100 homes of varying architectural styles had already been built when the Florida land boom collapsed, halting construction. Tris Speaker, manager of the Cleveland Indians, was reputedly one of the early Cleveland Heights's homeowners. (Lakeland Public Library.)

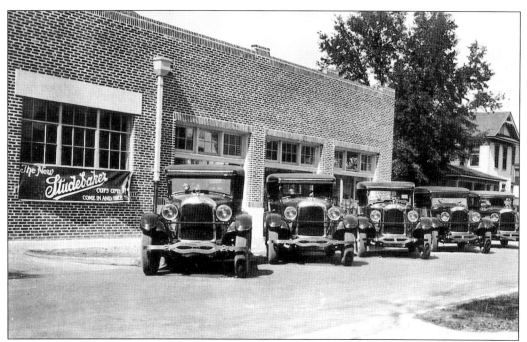

In 1912, poor road conditions forced motorists driving from Lakeland to Auburndale to make a 40-mile detour. A trip to New York from Lakeland that took only 10 days was considered remarkable. In 1916, there were fewer than 1,000 automobiles in all of Polk County. As roads improved, however, more people saw automobile ownership as desirable. With that change in attitude, several businesses soon offered residents a variety of car-buying opportunities. By 1925, the Studebaker dealership at 215 East Bay Street was urging customers, "The new Studebakers are here. Come in and see." In 1938, the Rocker Motor Company used a similar promotion to attract buyers, advertising "A Big New DeSoto Come See It." (Lakeland Public Library.)

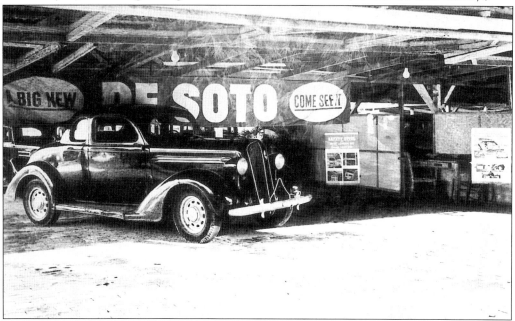

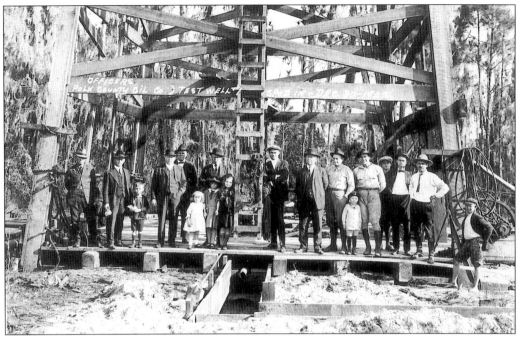

While it may have been an unlikely site for a family portrait, the officers of the Polk County Oil Company chose to pose for a photograph with their children on the platform of the company's test well. According to information written on the image negative by the Hinkley Studios' photographer, the well was "spud in" on December 30, 1922. Whether or not the well produced oil is unknown. Just a few years later, however, the men pictured in the bottom photograph reported striking oil instead of the water they were hoping to find. (Lakeland Public Library.)

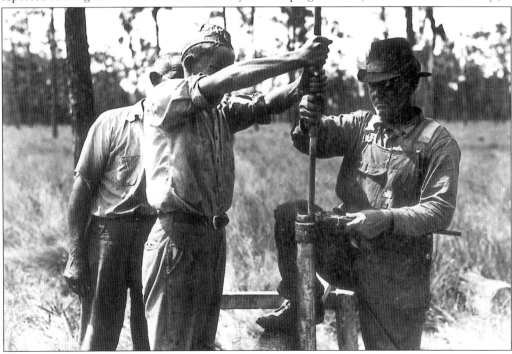

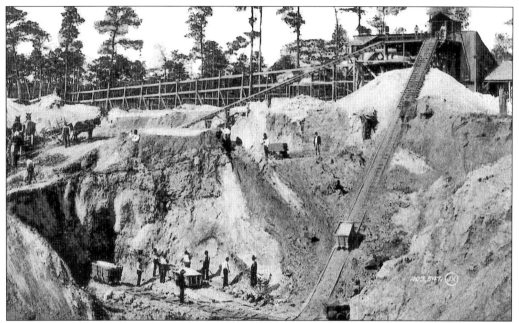

At the end of the 19th century, the discovery of large deposits of phosphate near Lakeland boded well for the future. Soon thousands of men were hard at work in the many phosphate pits in the surrounding area. Although companies used steam-powered equipment to extract the pebble phosphate from the ground, workers including many African-Americans wielded picks and shovels to perform much of the backbreaking labor as they moved the ore in handcarts. (Lakeland Public Library.)

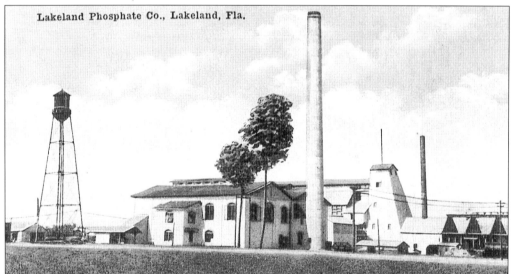

Although the phosphate mines were not located in Lakeland proper, most of the mining companies such as the Lakeland Phosphate Company were headquartered there. Columbus W. Deen, a well-known Lakeland businessman, served as president of the company in 1916, while H.E. Meminger, an electrical engineer and Auburn Institute graduate, was the manager. Producing phosphate for the European markets, the company also sold products such as "Natursown" to local farmers and growers. (Lakeland Public Library.)

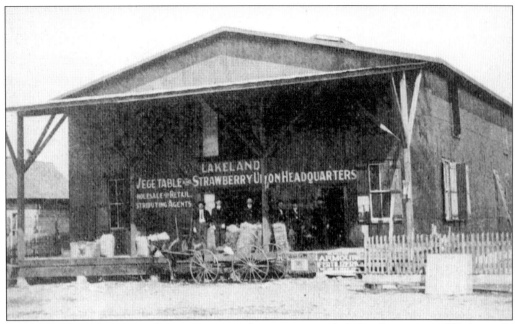

From its earliest days, agriculture was extremely important to Lakeland's economy. With nearly perfect weather that allowed year-round planting, tomatoes, beans, okra, eggplant, lettuce, cabbage, onions, and potatoes all proved abundant and profitable crops for truck farmers. Sugar cane, pineapples, peaches, and especially strawberries grew well. By 1888, it was reported that H.S. Galloway netted $600 from just one acre of berries. Six years later, Lakeland was shipping more strawberries than any other location in Florida. After farmers recognized the need to band together to ensure they all received fair and equitable prices for their crops, the Lakeland Vegetable and Strawberry Union was organized in 1897. It was developed to allow growers to deal from a position of strength brought about by unity and size. (Lakeland Public Library.)

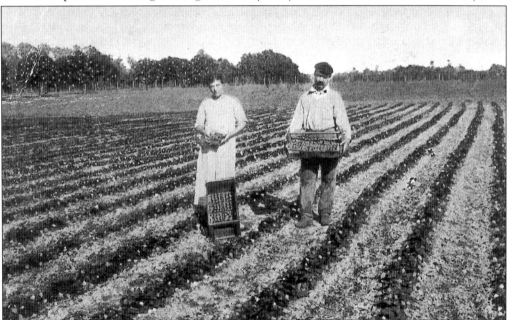

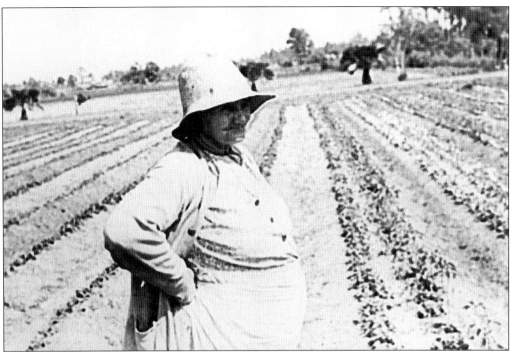

These photographs taken by Marion Wolcott in Lakeland in 1938 are but two of the more than 100,000 poignant images that Wolcott and her fellow photographers took while chronicling American life during the Depression. As illustrated by these striking images of strawberry pickers during hard times, Wolcott's work typically serves as a study in contrasts. While appearing to be old, the woman with her sun-parched face, look of futility, and heavy body is really of indeterminate age. She picks fruit in the Florida heat to help support a family ravaged by financial problems caused by forces beyond their control. The well-dressed young boy, however, sits in a relaxed pose enjoying a basket of freshly picked fruit. Feeding his family is not his concern. He may well have been the son of the farm's owner. (Library of Congress.)

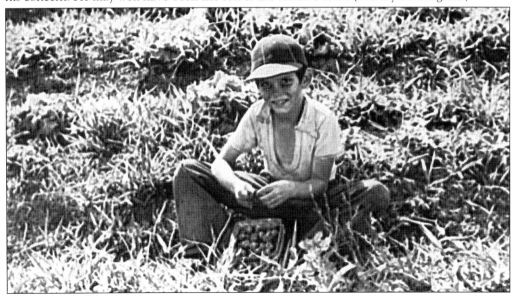

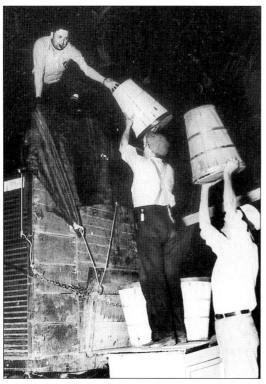

Farming was still Lakeland's number one industry in 1938. Produce needed to be picked within a finite length of time to prevent spoilage, making the harvest very much a family affair. Regardless of age or sex, anyone who could work the fields, did so. Although the area was segregated, at harvest time blacks and whites often worked together to get in the crops. Taken on April 12, 1938, this photograph shows a truck being loaded with the contents of 347 hampers of beans and squash destined for northern markets. (Lakeland Public Library.)

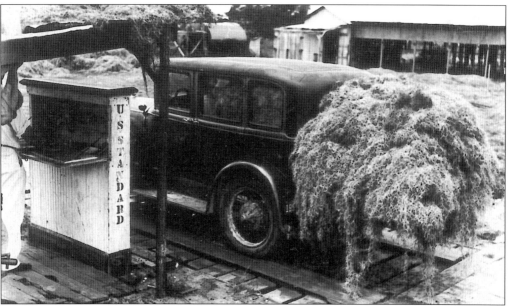

A thriving cottage industry during the 1920s and 1930s, the collection and processing of Spanish moss proved to be a welcome source of income during the Depression. Found hanging from live oak trees, the strands of moss, some as long as six feet in length, were collected and sold to processors. The material, in reality a plant and not a moss, was then cured and usually shipped north where it was used as stuffing for upholstery, automobile seats, and mattresses. (Lakeland Public Library.)

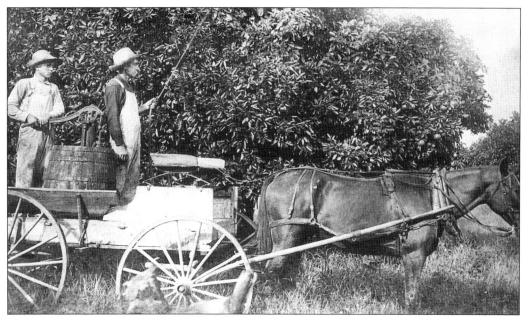

Workers at the C.M. Marsh grove diligently sprayed the citrus trees with chemicals to deter insects. Marsh owned a large grove and nursery on Lake Hollingsworth west of Ingraham Avenue and south of McDonald Street—the present site of Florida Southern College. Although Marsh is known as the developer of the seedless grapefruit, Edward Tison, the previous owner of the nursery, should probably receive the credit. (Lakeland Public Library.)

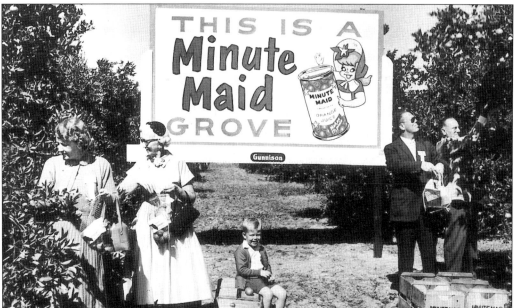

In the late 1940s, the Florida Foods Corporation began purchasing orange groves throughout Central Florida. Picked and shipped to a plant in Plymouth, the fruit was processed as frozen orange juice concentrate under the Minute Maid name. After the label achieved brand name recognition in supermarkets across the country, the company changed its name to the Minute Maid Company. Coca-Cola purchased the company in 1960. (Lakeland Public Library.)

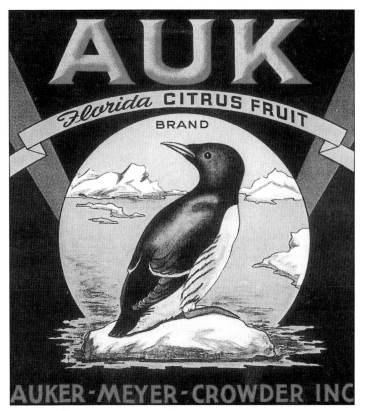

Frequently quite artistic, the fruit labels found on the ends of wooden packing crates were more than mere decoration. The labels advised buyers of several things—the brand name, type of fruit, place of origin, grade of the fruit, the grower, the packer, and the shipper. Highly collectible today, the labels were quite individualized, often featuring a favorite flower, bird, or even a member of the grower's family. In this case, the Auk label was obviously an effort to capitalize on the fame of the Detroit Tigers' submarine pitcher Elden Auker, a partner in Auker-Meyer-Crowder, Inc. as well as a member of the pennant-winning Tigers in both 1934 and 1935. (Lakeland Public Library.)

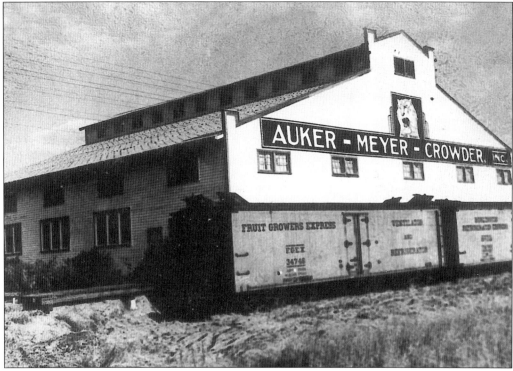

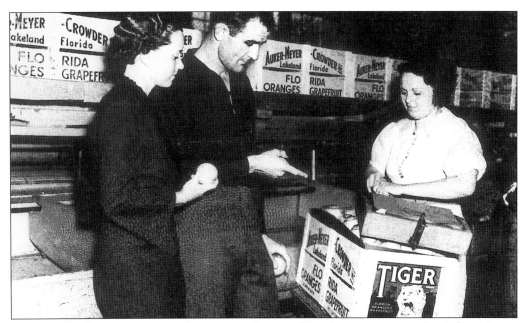

In more of a photo opportunity than an actual part of his job as a partner in the Auker-Meyer-Crowder citrus packinghouse, Elden Auker was pictured inspecting a crate of his Tiger-brand fruit in the mid-1930s. Over his ten-year sports career, Auker spent many months in Lakeland for spring training. While playing for the Boston Red Sox, the Detroit Tigers, and the St. Louis Browns, Auker compiled a record of 130 wins and 101 losses. (Lakeland Public Library.)

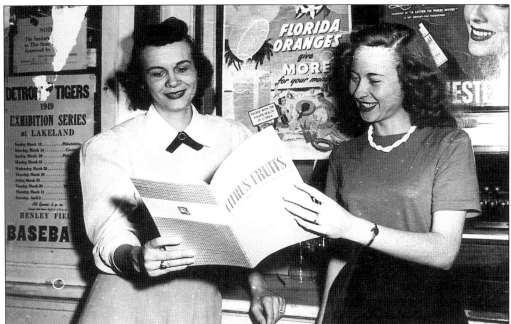

Another publicity shot combined two topics dear to the hearts of everyone in Lakeland—citrus and baseball. The two women are pictured perusing a publication about the citrus industry while standing in front of one poster advertising citrus and another listing the schedule for all of the exhibition games played by the Detroit Tigers. (Lakeland Public Library.)

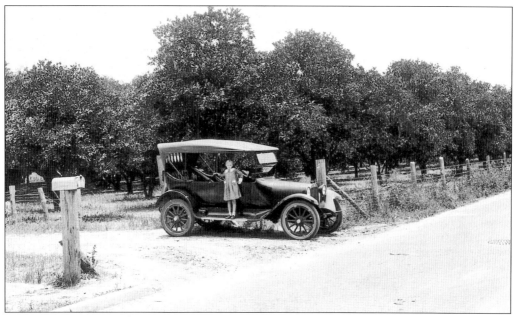

In 1915, Henry E. Pritchett moved his family to Lakeland from Jacksonville, where the 52-year-old entrepreneur had made his money in the naval stores industry. After relocating to Polk County, he went into the citrus business, purchasing groves in Lakeland and nearby Leesburg. The child standing on the running board of the automobile at his 60-acre Lakeland grove is probably one of his three daughters, Elizabeth, Thelma, or Effie. (Lakeland Public Library.)

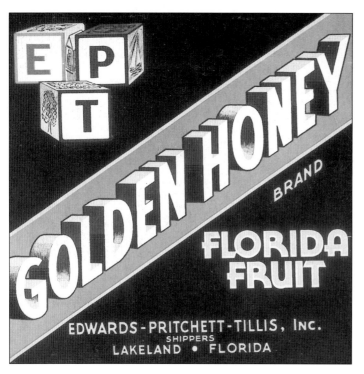

Fruit crate labels generally measured approximately nine inches square, as did this Golden Honey label of the Lakeland firm of Edwards, Pritchett, and Tillis, Inc. Labels were quite colorful, produced through a four-color process using light blue, yellow, red, and dark blue shades. Located in Tampa, Florida Growers Press printed most of the labels used by Florida citrus companies. The artfully designed labels, much like early billboards or advertising literature, served to attract northern fruit buyers. (Lakeland Public Library.)

Although Lakeland was situated right in the midst of Florida's citrus belt, not everyone owned an orange or grapefruit grove—or even had citrus trees in their backyard. There was an alternative, however. Innovations in the fruit processing industry meant a better tasting product as well as the year-round availability of citrus products. In June 1948, this eye-catching display of canned Florida fruit juice occupied the center of one aisle at the Publix supermarket in Lakeland. Adams-brand orange juice could be purchased for 19¢, while for a mere 17¢ shoppers could buy the same amount of Florida grapefruit juice. Ten years earlier, the Lakeland Junior Chamber of Commerce had offered free orange juice and tourist information from a stand designed to look just like a giant can of juice. (Lakeland Public Library.)

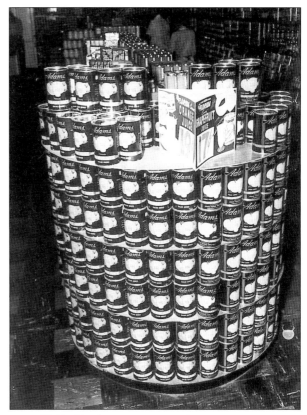

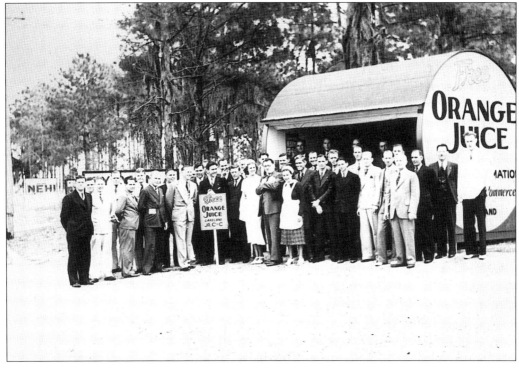

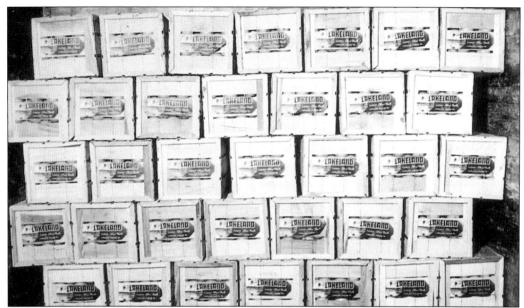

Much of the early history of citrus in Lakeland could be characterized as a conflict pitting individual growers against handlers, agents, and shippers. By the 1930s, prices for Florida citrus were at an all-time low; fruit was selling for little more than pennies a box. Growers faced mounting debts. The grading of the product was haphazard. Handlers and shippers controlled prices, with little order or stability to the industry. In response to the problems, the Florida legislature formed the Florida Citrus Commission in 1935 "to protect and enhance the quality and reputation of Florida citrus fruit and processed citrus products." By 1994–1995, the estimated value of citrus production to the Polk County economy totaled almost $450 million. Today both the Florida Department of Citrus and Florida Citrus Mutual are headquartered in Lakeland. (Lakeland Public Library.)

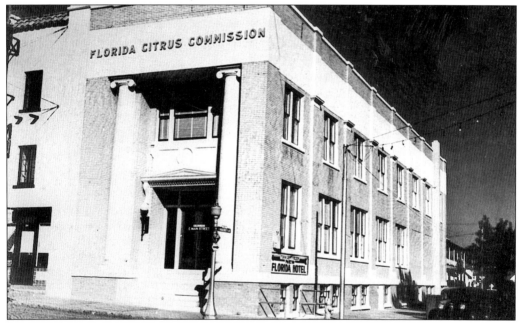

Six
HAVING FUN

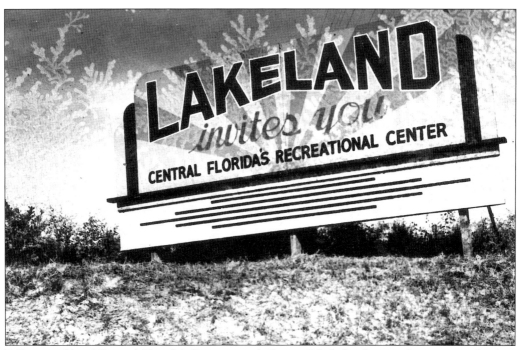

Billing itself as "Central Florida's Recreational Center," Lakeland invited visitors in the late 1930s to enjoy the many opportunities that the community offered for having fun. A tour of a garden filled with flowers in bloom was offset by a ride along a scenic drive. Golf played on the rolling links of an 18-hole course, a game of shuffleboard, or a lawn bowling match awaited the less sedentary individual. Fishing, boating, and water sports of all kinds competed for the visitor's time with the chance to watch a major league baseball game during spring training. And if the visitor encountered one of the few periods of inclement weather, a first-run movie at one of Lakeland's ornate movie palaces could be followed by a trip to the ice cream parlor. Lakeland offered something enjoyable for everyone. (Lakeland Public Library.)

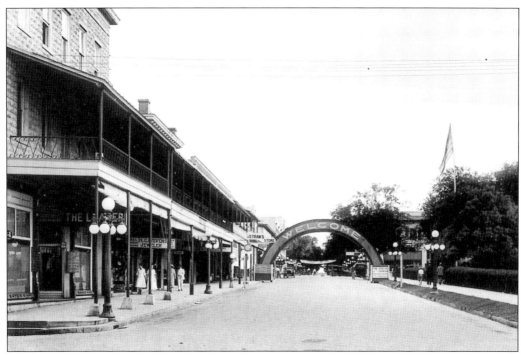

Lakeland was serious about showing visitors a warm reception. In fact, when the United Confederate Veterans held a reunion in Lakeland on November 1, 1914, the town went so far as to erect a welcoming arch that spanned Kentucky Avenue between Main and Rose Streets. Illuminated by hundreds of electric lights, the arch remained in place for several years as a distinctive reminder of the community's propensity for hospitality. (Lakeland Public Library.)

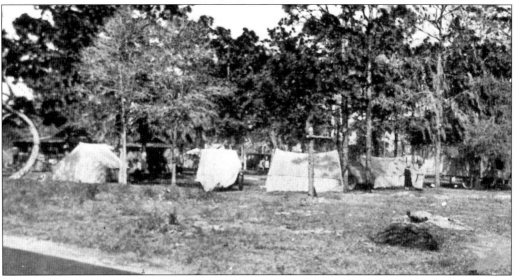

Visitors to Lakeland were nothing new, however. A souvenir edition of the *Lakeland News* in 1905 boasted that the town was "a great winter resort, being filled with tourists every winter." As automobile ownership became more prevalent, many visitors packed their cars and trailers with tents, household goods, and tinned foods. By 1931, Lakeland offered four tourist camps for the so-called "tin-can tourists." (Lakeland Public Library.)

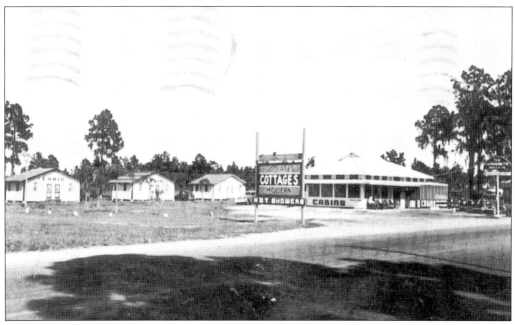

Tourist cabins such as the Alstates Cottages provided slightly more upscale accommodations, more privacy, and the added inducement of hot showers. Lakeland regarded tourists as more than just a temporary economic opportunity. The *City Directory* advised, "Every tourist is a potential permanent resident, and it is sought to make the visitors feel that the attitude of the people here is friendly and hospitable." (Lakeland Public Library.)

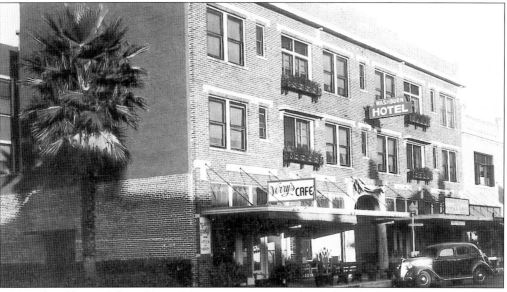

Although still not of the caliber of the Terrace or New Florida hotels, the Washburn Hotel was the next step up on the way to luxurious lodging. Built by Harry Washburn in 1923 at a cost of $125,000, the hotel on South Tennessee Avenue offered the additional opportunity for breakfast served from 7 until 10 a.m. at Verry's Cafe on the first floor. A lack of profitability led to the closing and eventual demolition of the structure, also known as the Gilbert-Washburn Hotel, in 1996. (Lakeland Public Library.)

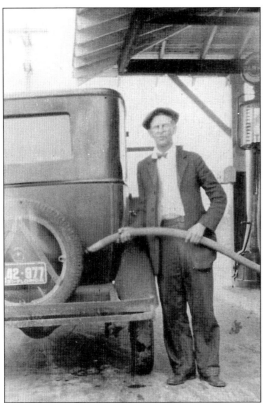

There was no such thing as self-service for the customers of C.A. Hayes, the proprietor of Hayes Villa. More than happy to pump the gasoline for his customers, Mr. Hayes was obviously a man intent on taking advantage of every economic opportunity presented by visitors to Lakeland and Central Florida in general. His entrepreneurial empire sold gasoline for the motorist's vehicle, advertised the rental of cottages for tourists who needed a place to stay, sold Celo soft drinks to the thirsty, and offered home-cooked barbecue for the hungry. In short, Hayes Villa provided the equivalent of one-stop shopping in 1931. (Lakeland Public Library.)

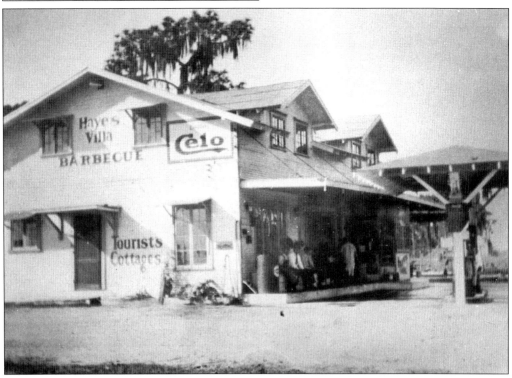

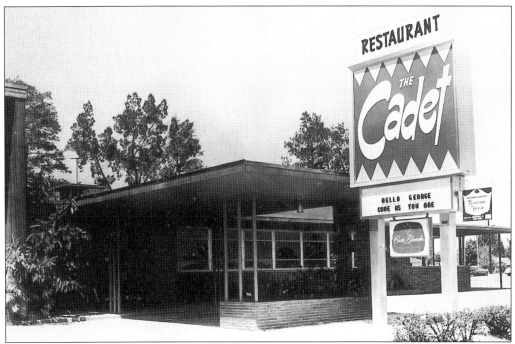

Lakeland offered a variety of places to eat. During World War II, the Cadet, a local restaurant situated across from Municipal Airport Number One, advertised, "Servicemen, the Cadet welcomes you." A few years later, the marquee welcomed "George" and advised him to "come as you are." There seemed to be just one popular choice when it came to beverages, however. Manufactured by a Chicago company, Dad's Old Fashioned Root Beer was famous for its foam. Available in 12-ounce bottles, Dad's could also be purchased in a half-gallon "Papa" size, a 32-ounce "Mama" amount, and various "Junior" portions. Since Lakeland was situated in Polk County with alcoholic beverages legally unavailable until 1963, the ice-cold beer sold with the hot chili and hamburgers at this restaurant was obviously root beer. (Lakeland Public Library.)

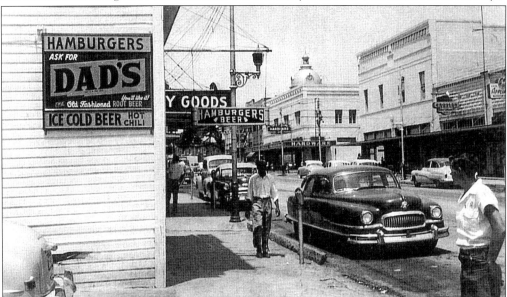

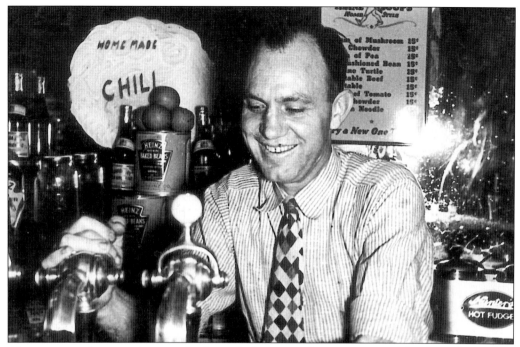

Almost every drugstore in town had a soda fountain where visitors and local residents alike could enjoy a light lunch or just a delicious snack. And of course, the one thing they all had in common was the soda jerk who could turn a concoction of milk, chocolate syrup, and vanilla ice cream into a frothy, ice-cold milkshake or an ice cream float. Jewett's had someone special behind its counter. Dick Trawick was more than just a store employee—he was a local celebrity. Trawick was so popular with his customers that they paid his way to the Rose Bowl game on New Year's Day in 1938. Much to the dismay of the avid University of Alabama football fan, the final score was 13-0, in favor of California. (Lakeland Public Library.)

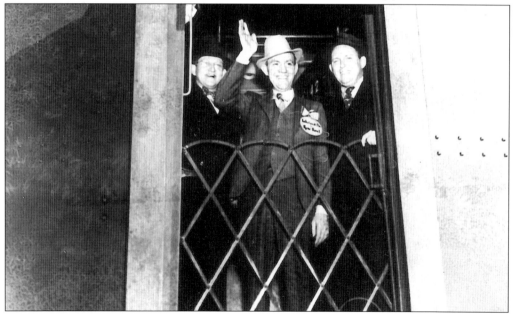

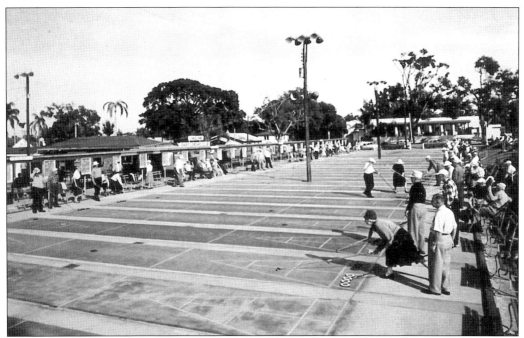

By 1926, the Lakeland Tourist Club listed on its rolls a total of 1,625 members from all over the world. In exchange for dues of just $1 per year, the organization offered ladies' afternoon parties and a Chautauqua series, as well as educational, literary, and musical programs. There were also dances, bridge and euchre games, and theatre outings. Outdoor activities included motorcades, fishing, golf, miniature golf, tennis, horseshoes, and roque. Shuffleboard and lawn bowling were two activities whose popularity continued into the 1940s, 1950s, and 1960s. The sign at the Lakeland Lawn Bowling Club entrance advised participants, "Enjoy Yourself—It's Later Than You Think." (Lakeland Public Library.)

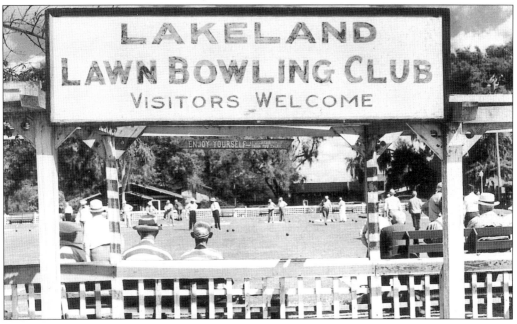

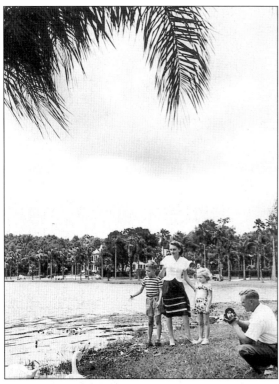

Even during the town's very early days, promotional materials touted the scenic beauty of the area, referring to Lakeland as "the Lovely City of Lakes." With ten major bodies of water, as well as several smaller ones from which to choose, both residents and visitors had plenty of opportunities to enjoy the natural beauty of their surroundings. Howard Hutchens used his movie camera to record the interaction between his family and the swans at Lake Morton during the 1950s. (Lakeland Public Library.)

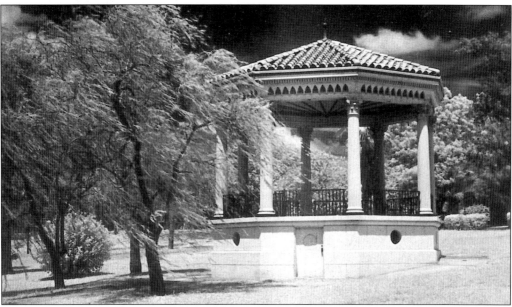

Complete with a barrel-tile roof, Greek columns, and iron railing, a circular bandstand graced the southeast side of Lake Mirror. Although there are no people visible in this 1948 photograph of the bandstand and its surrounding parkland, this was an unusual circumstance, since Lake Mirror Park had been a popular area until closed in the early 1950s to make way for a road. Thanks to the combined efforts of the city and local preservationists, today the park has been recreated as a "community gathering place." (Lakeland Public Library.)

Whether standing on the banks of Lake Morton at sunset or along the Lake Mirror Promenade, fishermen vied for the opportunity to catch "a big one" for either sport or dinner. Ranging in size from the one-half-mile circumference of Lakes Mirror and Morton to Lake Parker, covering a 21-square-mile area, the community's various lakes offered ample chances to do a little fishing. The 1905 souvenir edition of the *Lakeland News* proudly offered an early description. "These lakes, whose waters are so pure that a careful analysis has declared them excellent for drinking purposes, abound in fish of the highest quality, and afford excellent sport to the devotees of Walton, as well as being a constant source of pleasure to the residents." (Lakeland Public Library.)

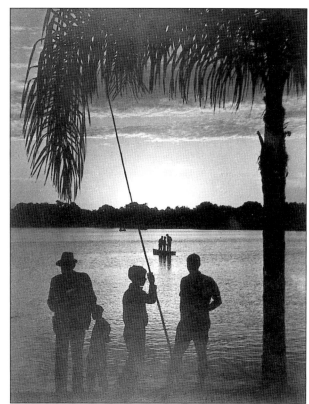

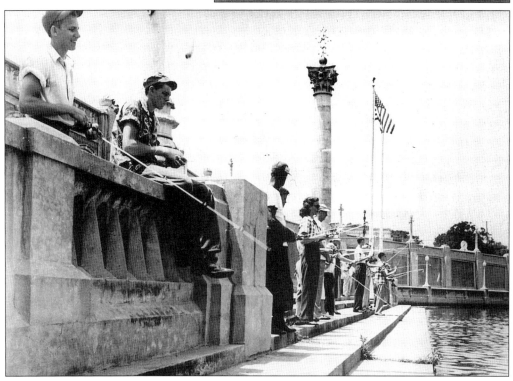

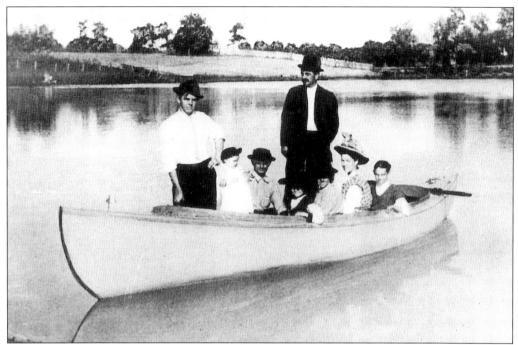

These two photographs, separated in time by just half a century, show a marked difference in sporting attire. In the upper image, the entire family posed for a photograph while canoeing on Lake Beulah. With the exception of one child, all wore hats to shield them from the sun; the hats, however, were not beachwear but rather everyday dress. Potentially endangering the stability of the entire situation as they stand in the back of the canoe, the family patriarch appears most elegant in his black suit and matching fedora; the eldest son is only slightly less formally dressed. The two young women in the lower photo were much more practically attired as they demonstrated their skills at water skiing. (Lakeland Public Library.)

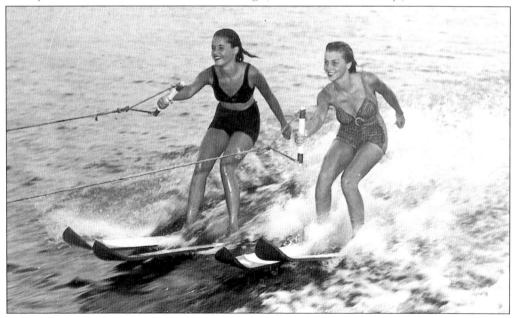

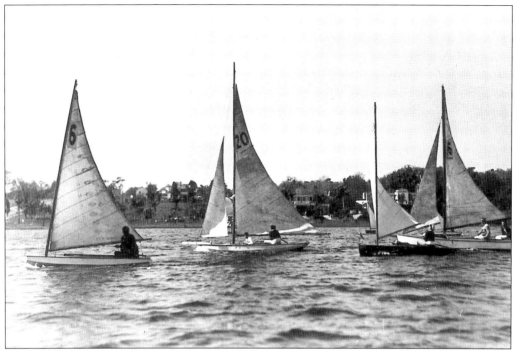

During the 1920s, Francis Beach was a popular swimming and boating spot on the south shore of Lake Hollingsworth. Built by J.L. Francis in 1915, the area was the site of weekly dances during the summertime. Founded in 1949, the Lakeland Ski Club held its annual water skiing tournaments on Lake Hollingsworth, while the lake was also the frequent location for sailboat regattas, boat parades, and competitions. (Lakeland Public Library.)

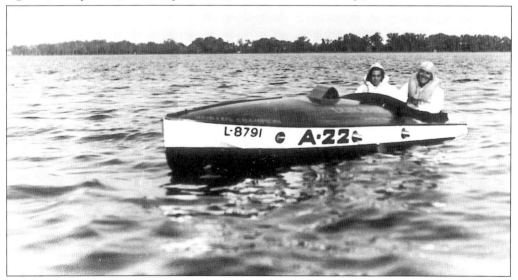

Hoping to break one of the many records set on Lake Hollingsworth's circular course, these two men took part in the 1936 power boat races. Today drivers come to Lakeland from all over the world to take part in the annual Orange Cup Regatta hydroplane competition. Thousands of spectators line the shores of Lake Hollingsworth for the event that is held each spring around the Easter weekend. (Lakeland Public Library.)

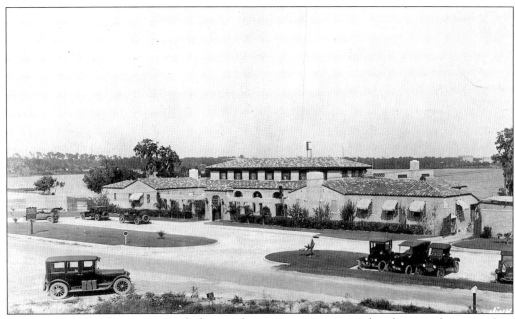

Located on the former site of the Fred W. Pope citrus packinghouse, this sprawling Spanish-style structure became the Cleveland Heights Club, the centerpiece of H.A. Stahl's Cleveland Heights golf course community. Overlooking Lake Hollingsworth, the building stood vacant for several years following the collapse of the land boom of the 1920s. After the city took both the Cleveland Heights's golf course and its clubhouse for delinquent taxes, the property on Lake Hollingsworth Drive was leased to the Lakeland Yacht and Country Club in 1935. Sixty-two-passenger buses brought prospective buyers from as far away as Tampa and St. Petersburg to tour the home sites and 18-hole golf course of the Cleveland Heights development. (Lakeland Public Library.)

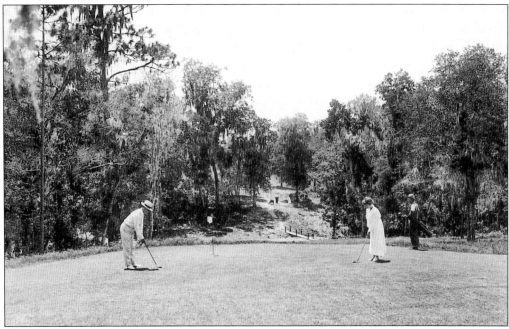

Every spring, hundreds of people, tourists and locals alike, would visit C.F. Smith's Lakeland Heights estate for a glimpse of the beautiful display of multi-colored tulips. The lush gardens and windmill were reminiscent of a scene in the Dutch countryside. The *Lakeland Ledger* featured this image on its front page on March 11, 1947, thanks to the skills of photographer Dan Sanborn. (Lakeland Public Library.)

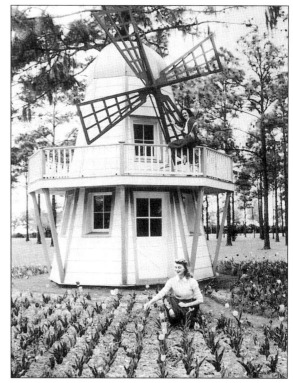

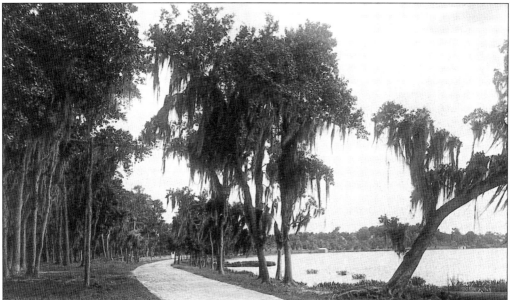

While they may have sounded poetic, the names given to Lakeland's many lakes frequently had a logical basis. Lake Beulah honored Miss Beulah Wentz, an attractive visitor. Lake Parker was named for Streety Parker, a former resident, and Lake Morton in recognition of John P. Morton, purchaser of the surrounding land. Both Lake Hollingsworth and the picturesque drive encircling it took their names from that of an early settler who farmed the area around the lake. (Lakeland Public Library.)

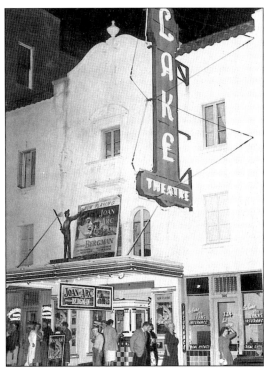

During the 1940s, long before anyone dreamed of 24-screen cinematic megaplexes, Lakeland's moviegoers had their choice of several local indoor movie theatres—all of which offered first-run movies. This 1948 photograph of the Lake Theatre on Main Street reveals that the feature performance of the day was *Joan of Arc*, starring Ingrid Bergman and José Ferrer. (Lakeland Public Library.)

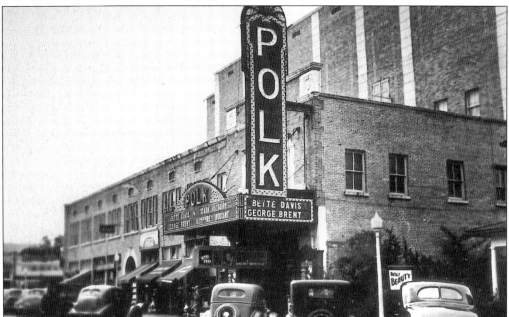

Built in 1928, the Polk Theatre was known as an atmospheric theatre because of a ceiling that featured fluffy clouds, twinkling stars, and sunrise/sunset effects. The Polk did more than just show films; vaudeville acts, community programs, and celebrity performances also drew patrons. An air-conditioning system so strong that it caused lights to dim all over Lakeland may have been an additional attraction during warm Florida weather. Beautifully restored in 1999, the Polk Theatre is once again a cinematic jewel. (Lakeland Public Library.)

As these views of the Palace Theatre attest, going to the movies was a popular activity in the 1940s. Tickets that cost only a quarter for adults and ten cents for children encouraged people of all ages to patronize films promising "Murder, Romance, Action." Adults enjoyed an evening out; dating teenagers sought the privacy of the darkened balcony. Kids hoped to see their favorite movie hero triumph over the bad guys. And of course, if the movie concessions stand with its popcorn, candy, and soft drinks did not offer enough in the way of sustenance, there was always a trip to the Palace Sweet Shoppe after the movie ended. (Lakeland Public Library.)

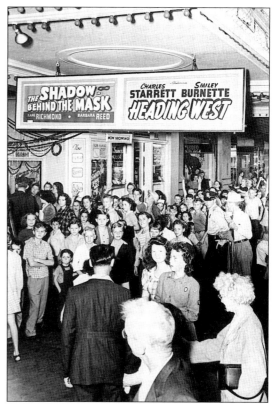

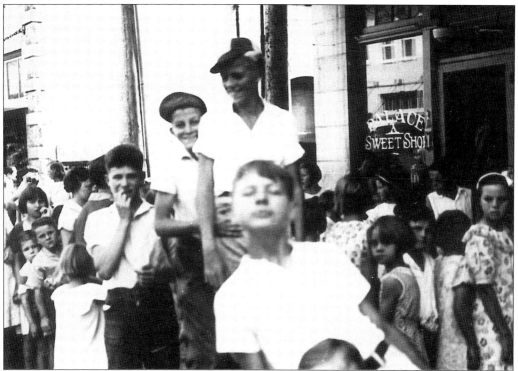

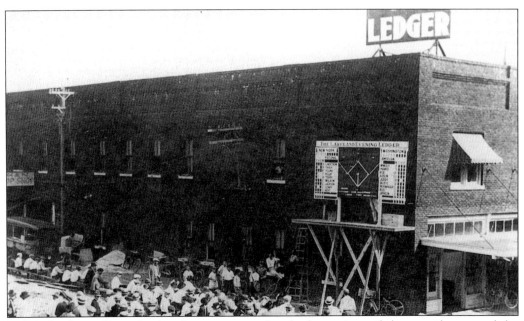

Before the days of live play-by-play sportscasts, fans had to wait until the next day to read the results of baseball games. For more immediate accounts, crowds gathered outside of the *Lakeland Ledger* offices where staff members monitored the games via wire service reports and then reenacted the action. This picture was taken during the 1924 World Series as the New York Giants held a two-to-zero lead over the Washington Senators. Although the Giants won this game, the Senators ultimately won the Series. (Lakeland Public Library.)

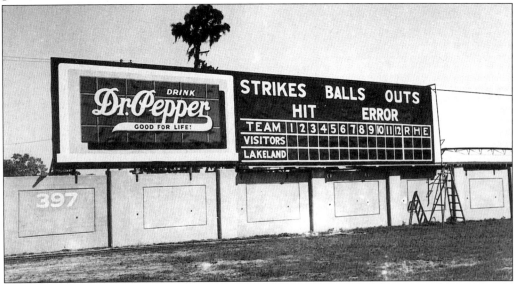

Henley Park, the city's first municipal ballpark, was built in 1925 and later named for Dr. Clare Henley, a leading proponent of baseball in Lakeland. Awarded landmark status in 1997, the ballpark is used today for local amateur athletics, as well as by the Florida Southern College team. Following its construction, however, it served as home to the Cleveland Indians during spring training. After their departure in 1928, Lakeland sorely missed having a "home team." (Lakeland Public Library.)

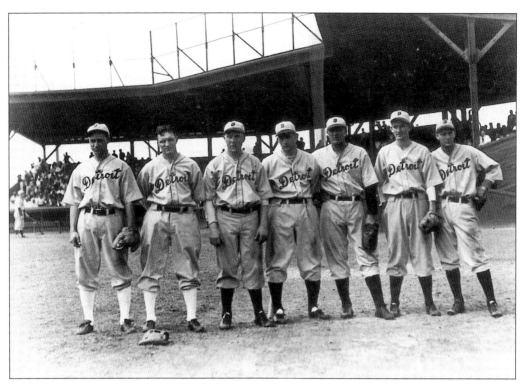

Using WPA workers, the city set to work putting its municipal field in shape in the hope of attracting another team. Residents rejoiced when in 1934 city fathers forged with the Detroit Tigers what would become the longest continuous spring training relationship in the major leagues. Although the team no longer uses Henley Field, now playing its games at Lakeland's Joker Marchant Stadium, baseball fans still turn out to support their team—the Tigers. (Lakeland Public Library.)

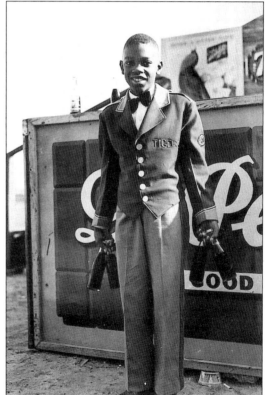

Spring training in Florida was, and still is, big business as cities vied to attract and keep baseball teams. Local residents were not the only ones to attend the games. Many seasonal visitors from northern states made it a point to support their home teams during spring training in Florida, adding additional economic impact. Spring training also provided jobs for local youngsters who worked as concessionaires, selling peanuts, popcorn, and soft drinks in the stands. (Lakeland Public Library.)

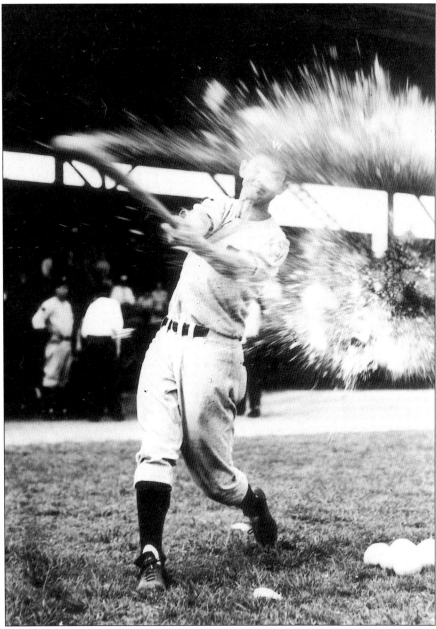

Hank Greenberg gave new meaning to the term "Grapefruit League" when he slugged some of Florida's world famous grapefruit "outta the park" in March 1941. Greenberg was always a favorite of Lakeland's baseball fans, who avidly cheered him each year when the Detroit Tigers came to town for spring training. When America entered World War II, Greenberg left baseball to enter the Army Air Forces, saying, "My country comes first." After his return from military service in 1945, the two-time winner of the American League's most valuable player award returned to his baseball career. On September 8, 1945, Lakeland's citizens demonstrated their affection for "Hammerin' Hank" as the Lakeland Chamber of Commerce made him the town's honorary president for life. Upon his induction into the Baseball Hall of Fame, Greenberg was described as "one of baseball's greatest right-handed batters." (Lakeland Public Library.)